PERSEVERANCE PAYS

WINNING THE CROWN OF LIFE

ENCOURAGEMENT FROM THE EPISTLE OF JAMES

SCOTT CRAWFORD

PERSEVERANCE PAYS

Winning the Crown of Life

©Copyright 2011 by Scott Crawford

Word of Truth Press
Asheville, NC

www.wordoftruthclass.org

teacher@wordoftruthclass.org

All rights reserved. No portion of this book may be reproduced without the written permission of the author except as provided by USA copyright law.

Unless otherwise noted, all scripture quotations are from the King James Version.

CONTENTS

ACKNOWLEDGEMENTS iii

INTRODUCTION 1

CHAPTER 1 TRIUMPH THROUGH TRIALS 7

CHAPTER 2 WISDOM AND FAITH 13

CHAPTER 3 EVIL, SIN, AND DEATH 19

CHAPTER 4 GOOD GIFTS FROM ABOVE 27

CHAPTER 5 EARS OPEN – MOUTH SHUT 37

CHAPTER 6 HEARING AND DOING 51

CHAPTER 7 PURE RELIGION 63

CHAPTER 8 HONOR WHO – RICH OR POOR 75

CHAPTER 9 THE ROYAL LAW 83

CHAPTER 10 FAITH – ALIVE OR DEAD 89

CHAPTER 11 MATURE FAITH – IT WORKS 99

CHAPTER 12 THE PERFECT MAN 107

CHAPTER 13 THE BIG MOUTH 117

CHAPTER 14 WISE MEN 127

CHAPTER 15 LUST AND WAR 137

CHAPTER 16 WHO'S YOUR FRIEND 145

CHAPTER 17 HUMILITY'S PATH 153

CHAPTER 18 WATCH WHAT YOU SAY 165

CHAPTER 19 LIFE IS SHORT 173

CHAPTER 20 THE DECEIT OF WEALTH 181

CHAPTER 21 THE LORD IS COMING 189

CHAPTER 22 THE JUDGE KNOWS ALL 197

CHAPTER 23 MANIPULATION 205

CHAPTER 24 THE POWER OF PRAYER AND PRAISE 211

CHAPTER 25 LOVE RESTORES 221

CHAPTER 26 ENCOURAGEMENT 229

ACKNOWLEDGEMENTS

First and foremost I wish to thank my gracious loving Lord for His manifold blessings! Without Him I would be nothing, like a ship without a sail!

I love and appreciate my lovely wife Betsy for her proofreading and suggestions (however, I am responsible for any errors). Her love, support, and encouragement have aided me greatly!

I wish to thank my parents, Jim and Anniece Crawford, for their steadfast love and support. I am truly blessed to have such wonderful parents!

Marty Cauley skillfully helped with the layout as well as giving numerous ideas and support. I love and appreciate him!

Over the years Lewis Schoettle has encouraged me greatly. His love for the Lord and me is greatly appreciated!

There are many others I could name who have helped me along the way to understand the Lord and His Word. These are too numerous to mention, but I am certainly grateful for their influence.

Perseverance Pays

INTRODUCTION

Thank you for joining me as we study God's Word together! It is a great privilege to share this book with you. My goal is to help you better understand what God is saying through James. The book of James is a much loved book in the Bible. Many have turned to James for encouragement as well as instruction in righteousness. God certainly blessed us when He inspired James to pen his five chapters. As we study this great book together, my prayer is that God will grant you wisdom and understanding. I have taken time to aid you in your endeavor for wisdom by providing some questions for thoughtful study at the end of each chapter. You can use them personally or for group study. I encourage you to get the most you possibly can from this study. As you will learn, God has great things in store for us as we persevere in the faith! Please be encouraged as you meditate upon the message of James.

Please join me now as we explore some introductory remarks concerning James. Knowing this introductory material will help us better understand his message.

Author: The Epistle of James was written by the half brother of our Lord Jesus Christ. James was a significant leader in the Jerusalem church (Acts 12:17; 15:13; 21:18). Interestingly, James along with his brothers and sisters did not believe in the Lord Jesus for eternal life prior to His resurrection (John 7:5), but after the resurrection, they believed in Him (Acts 1:14). James is named in 1 Cor 15:7 as being one to whom the Lord Jesus Christ revealed Himself after His resurrection.

Date: Evidence supports that James was the very first New Testament book written. Although some date the writing of the book between 45-50 AD, it is possible that it was penned as early as 34 or 35 AD! If the crucifixion was in 33 AD, then James was written right on the heels of the events described in the Gospels. However, James was written before the Gospels were penned since the earliest proposed date for one of the Gospels is around 50 AD. Following James, the next New Testament book written was most likely Galatians, around 49 AD.

Audience: James 1:1 indicates that the intended recipients were the *twelve tribes scattered abroad*. Because of the early date of the epistle, the recipients were Christians who were ethnic Jews. These Jewish Christians had been living in Jerusalem in a communal state (Acts 4:32-35) but due to persecution, (Acts 8:1) had been scattered. Although Jewish by natural birth, these believers were first and foremost Christians – members of the body of Christ (1 Cor 12:12; 2 Cor 5:17).

Not only is this historical setting interesting, it is also very helpful as we study this first New Testament book. The persecution experienced by early believers was devastating. They had sold all of their earthly possessions with the proceeds being distributed among the church so that everyone had what they needed. However, as persecution came, they then were forced to flee Jerusalem to various places with little sustenance. This historical setting should also help us put the words of James in context. It should make his epistle come alive! James wrote as a concerned pastor to believers in numerous places who had experienced this great persecution. While Americans do not presently face this intensity of persecution, we should heed

Introduction

James' words with great anticipation. Persecution relative to the Christian life is to be expected and received with joy (James 1:2)!

Literary style: Some have explained James to be a Midrash on the Sermon on the Mount. A Midrash is a Jewish commentary which helps fill in the gaps of understanding. Notice the following similarities between James and the Sermon on the Mount:

James	Matthew
1:2	5:10-12
1:4	5:48
1:5; 5:15	7:7-12
1:9	5:3
2:13	5:7; 6:14-15
3:17-18	5:9
4:4	6:24
4:10	5:3-5
4:11	7:1-2
5:2	6:19
5:10	5:12
5:12	5:33-37

James' literary structure seeks to enforce his overarching theme: **enduring patiently during the trials of life brings great reward – perseverance pays!** His theme will be easily observed by the diligent reader. It should also be noted that James is a gifted speaker and writer. His style is both abrupt and vivid. His leadership is evidenced by his tone and authority. James also is a very practical book with effective illustrations and practical admonitions (warnings or cautions). We must keep in mind this style of communication as we draw lessons from James. Most likely, this epistle was simply a written sermon which was distributed to Christians throughout the region.

Purpose: As noted above, the theme is perseverance pays. Writing to Christians who had been scattered (likely sometime after the death of Stephen in Acts 7), James seeks to both encourage and warn them. While persecutions come and go, we all need to be reminded daily of the words of our Lord. Day to day living will present problems; quarrels and disputes arise (4:1). They must be dealt with in a loving and peaceable manner (5:7-10) especially in the context of the New Testament Church.

Following is an outline of the epistle of James. Please review it so you will have a general understanding of how the book is structured. You will find James has a salutation, prologue, and theme. The body of the epistle has three parts followed by the epilogue. I believe James was very purposeful when he wrote as he did. Take a moment to familiarize yourself with this outline as we will refer back to it as we study James together.

Outline[1]

1. Salutation: (1:1)
2. Prologue: Properly Respond to Trials (1:2-18)
    a. Welcome trials (1:2-11)
    b. Do not accuse or criticize God for trials (1:12-18)
3. Theme: Endure Patiently (1:19-20)

---

[1]This outline has been adapted from Hodges outline.

Introduction

4. Body of the Epistle: Develop Godly Character (1:21-5:6)
    a. By Being Swift to Hear (1:21-26)
        i. Do more than simply listen (1:21-27)
        ii. Go beyond mere morality (2:1-13)
        iii. Have active faith (2:14-26)
    b. By Being Slow to Speak (3:1-18)
        i. The tongue is dangerous and can lack wisdom (3:1-12)
        ii. Holy living is the best way to display wisdom (3:13-18)
    c. By Being Slow to Wrath (4:1-5:6)
        i. Worldliness creates wrath (4:1-5)
        ii. Humility cures wrath (4:6-5:6)
            1. Humility brings repentance from sin (4:6-10)
            2. Humility restrains speech (4:11-12)
            3. Humility is reluctant to boast (4:13-5:6)
5. Epilogue: Persevere in Trials to the End (5:7-20)
    a. Perseverance will be rewarded (5:7-11)
    b. Prayer helps produce perseverance (5:12-20)

Note on Faith: Some have questioned James' authenticity and inclusion in the New Testament – Martin Luther being one. Since James was written prior to Paul's ministry and writings, we should conclude Paul was very aware of James' epistle and teaching. Paul knew James well and had several encounters with him (cf. Acts 15:13). Paul and James do not contradict each other. In fact, they both have the same teachings regarding faith. By definition, **faith is the persuasion that something is true; Biblically, it is the inward conviction that what God has said is true.** The justification by faith Paul discusses in Romans Chapters

3-5 is relative to the **gift of eternal life**. In Ephesians 2:8-9 Paul says faith alone – absent of works – saves relative to the gift of **eternal life**. The justification by faith and works James discusses in Chapter 2 is relative to **eternal reward.** Both Paul and James wrote to Christians to encourage them to have an active and vibrant faith – not one that is dead and fruitless (Eph 4-5; Col 3). Neither Paul nor James promotes introspection amongst believers to "test" and see if they have the gift of eternal life. Rather, they encourage believers (those who possess the gift of eternal life) to live holy lives that are pleasing to God which produce fruit – righteous works. Hence, we should not look to our works to prove our **relationship** with God. Belief in (reliant trust) the promise of God settles this matter fully and completely (John 3:16; 6:47; Eph 2:8-9; 1 John 5:13). Instead of looking at our works to continually prove our relationship with God, we should look to our works to determine our **fellowship** with God. If we are conducting our lives according to God's Word (being hearers and doers), we are assured that we are in fellowship with Him having a vibrant faith which is alive for all to see. According to James and Paul (James 1:12; Col 3:23-25), such perseverance will result in eternal reward– Perseverance Pays!

CHAPTER 1
TRIUMPH THROUGH TRIALS

James 1:1-4, 12

¹*James, a servant of God and of the Lord Jesus Christ, to the twelve tribes which are scattered abroad, greeting. ²My brethren, count it all joy [full joy or pure joy] when ye fall into divers [various] temptations [trials or testings]; ³Knowing [you know] this, that the trying of your faith worketh patience [endurance or perseverance]. ⁴But let patience [endurance or perseverance] have her perfect [complete] work, that ye may be perfect [complete] and entire [intact], wanting [lacking] nothing.*

¹²*Blessed [happy or fortunate] is the man that endureth temptation [trials or testings]: for when he is tried, he shall receive the crown of life, which the Lord hath promised to them that love him.*

Writing to Christians scattered throughout the Middle East, James greets them in love and immediately tells them to welcome the trials in their lives! How odd – or is it? Consider Jesus' words:

> ³ Blessed are the poor in spirit: for theirs is the kingdom of heaven. ⁴ Blessed are they that mourn:

for they shall be comforted. ⁵ Blessed are the meek: for they shall inherit the earth. ⁶ Blessed are they which do hunger and thirst after righteousness: for they shall be filled. ⁷ Blessed are the merciful: for they shall obtain mercy. ⁸ Blessed are the pure in heart: for they shall see God. ⁹ Blessed are the peacemakers: for they shall be called the children of God. ¹⁰ Blessed are they which are persecuted for righteousness' sake: for theirs is the kingdom of heaven. ¹¹ Blessed are ye, when men shall revile you, and persecute you, and shall say all manner of evil against you falsely, for my sake. ¹² **Rejoice, and be exceeding glad: for great is your reward in heaven**: for so persecuted they the prophets which were before you. [Emphasis mine] (Matt 5:3-12)

    James was telling these every day believers (moms, dads, children, employees, slaves, etc.) to heed the words of Jesus. We should rejoice in the face of trials. This seems so counter intuitive. Most of us want to escape trials or testing. We want the easy and good life. Our culture – even our religious culture – has taught us the "good life" is a sign of blessing from God! However, this is not the teaching of the New Testament and surely not of James. Right off the bat James tells us to rejoice in trials – not for the trials but **in** the trials.
    But why? Why should we look forward or rejoice in something difficult? Why should we have pure joy for a life that yields trials and testings? Since we have been saved from the lake of fire, should not everything be okay, and life be a bed of roses

full of material abundance and riches? Well, according to James we should anticipate trouble and allow it to change us.

James tells his readers how stress in their life has divine purpose! In fact, trials are divinely ordered for every Christian. Stress in our lives causes us to seek help from our Lord. It causes us to work hard and endure. God is pleased when we labor by faith. By faith, we know trials are causing us to become mature in our faith. Hence, faith is perfected or completed or brought to its desired goal when we endure the trials of life. When we are mature we will have full joy and fellowship with our Lord (cf. 1 John 1:4). When we are mature we will better understand His will and ways for us. If we refuse to mature, we will miss what God has in store for us. Hence, James' main point is to promote maturity among believers! Compare these truths with those revealed by the Apostle Peter in 1 Peter 1:6-8.

Happy and fortunate is the one who endures [with the proper motive and attitude] the various trials of life, especially any kind of religious persecution! Why or for what? Aren't we as Christians going to heaven anyway? Why doesn't God just take us there right away when we are first saved? Why should we be happy because we have it rough? Obviously there is more to the picture than simply going to heaven!?!? God must have something else in mind for us.

According to James, we should be happy for trials because they cause us to become mature. As we mature, we will learn to love the Lord and trust Him in every situation. Because of our faith and works of perseverance, we will be afforded a reward – *the crown of life*. In other words, perseverance pays! James, being the half brother of our Lord Jesus Christ, was very familiar with His teaching. Although James did not believe on the Lord

Jesus until after Jesus' resurrection, James most likely heard the Sermon on the Mount. In that sermon, Jesus said great reward in heaven would be the result for those who obeyed Him and suffered for Him while on earth (cf. Matt 5:11-12). Knowing this truth, James had taught it to his parishioners. In these opening verses, James reminds believers in Jesus Christ – those who have been forgiven and possess eternal life – that they have something to look forward to in heaven! Believers have the ability to store up treasure for themselves in heaven (cf. Matt 6:19-20). In fact, Jesus commanded us to do so! James is reminding us of our Lord's command to desire poverty on earth in order to have riches in heaven! The only way to do so is to walk through trials, for this is God's way. And we know His ways are higher than our ways!

With this understanding of James' opening thoughts, we should realize how much our Lord loves us. We should not think trials mean the Lord is angry with us. Quite the contrary, we need to anticipate trials with joy! We need to renew our minds (Rom 12:2) and be hearers and doers of the Word (James 1:22). If we do not take God at His Word, we are deceiving ourselves. God wants to richly bless us with reward and loving words of commendation. James' *crown of life* speaks of a quality of life in heaven. It also denotes a quality of life on earth which anticipates wealth and full joy in heaven. Peter mentioned this truth in 2 Peter 1:11 when he said abundant entrance into the kingdom would be ours if we persevered in the faith.

The promise of reward, specifically *the crown of life*, should cause us to pause for a moment. We must appreciate the regal nature of a *crown*. Those with crowns are noble rulers! Through James, God is showing us the noble position for which we have been created (cf. Gen 1:26-28; Heb 2:5-8)! Regality and nobility describe the future for faithful believers! Close knit, shared, intimate experiences with King Jesus will be afforded the overcoming Christian in Christ's coming kingdom (cf. Rev 2-3)! Thus, we must comprehend the significance of being awarded *the crown of life*! This reward is royal and majestic in nature. Earning this crown is much more than a token award. Paul understood the value of earning the *crown* when he wrote:

> [7] I have fought a good fight, I have finished *my* course, I have kept the faith: [8] Henceforth there is laid up for me a **crown** of righteousness, which the Lord, the righteous judge, shall give me at that day: and not to me only, but unto all them also that love his appearing.

The prospect of sitting beside King Jesus while assisting Him as a benevolent ruler in His kingdom is overwhelming! The glory we can share with Christ is astounding! Imagine being able to assist the Lord Jesus Christ as He administers compassionate justice upon the earth! Attaining this position is a most worthy pursuit for which we have been called (Eph 4:1; 1 Thes 2:12). Possessing *the crown of life* will change our lives for eternity!

With this knowledge our attitude should be positive; and our outlook should be bright, no matter the circumstances! Our Lord is doing all things for our good and for His glory! So rejoice in your trials looking for the maturity they bring. Draw close to the Lord, and then He will draw close to you (5:8). Humble yourself and God will exalt you (4:10). The tests God puts in our lives are for our good. He wants us to pass with flying colors so we can be rewarded with *the crown of life*!

DISCUSSION QUESTIONS AND IDEAS

- Is the Christian life supposed to be easy?
- Should I feel like God is upset with me when I experience trials?
- Should I be upset with God when people make fun of me for being a Christian?
- Why would God allow me to have troubles and trials in my life?
- How can I be happy or joyful when troubles come my way?
- What should be my motivation to continue being faithful to the Lord even in trials?
- Give an example of being rewarded for perseverance and obedience. Try to develop a story that interweaves trials and discouragement along with triumph in the end.
- Liken the "testing" we receive from God to tests given in school. The goal of testing is to determine the growth of knowledge a student experiences. Good test scores reveal a student who is prepared and ready for the test. Talk about how important it is to be ready for the "tests" so that we can be on "God's honor roll."

CHAPTER 2
WISDOM AND FAITH

James 1:5-11

⁵If any of you lack wisdom, let him ask of God, that giveth to all men liberally [bountifully], and upbraideth not[does not chide]; and it shall be given him. ⁶ But let him ask in faith, nothing wavering. For he that wavereth is like a wave of the sea driven with the wind and tossed. ⁷ For let not that man think that he shall receive any thing of the Lord. ⁸ A double minded man is unstable in all his ways. ⁹ Let the brother of low degree rejoice in that he is exalted: ¹⁰ But the rich, in that he is made low: because as the flower of the grass he shall pass away. ¹¹For the sun is no sooner risen with a burning heat, but it withereth the grass, and the flower thereof falleth, and the grace of the fashion of it perisheth: so also shall the rich man fade away in his ways.

Knowing the reality and severity of trials, James now advises us on how we should handle the trials – wisely. We must remember the reason for trials is to produce patience or endurance in us. As we endure trials, we can look forward to a reward – the *crown of life* (cf. v.12). This goal is a most worthwhile noble pursuit! Perseverance through trials results in a victorious Christian life which receives a reward from our Judge – the Lord Jesus Christ. Overcoming the trials and tribulations of our current journey is a great accomplishment! The Lord will not forget our labor of love (Heb 6:10). He will reward our perseverance (Heb 10:35). This fact is ever upon the mind of James, because his brother – the Master Teacher – made it a point to encourage faithful believers with the promise of reward (cf. Matt 5:12; Mark 10:28-31; Luke 6:35).

The moment we were born again (cf. 1:18; John 3:3) we received the life of God in our spirit. However, at that moment – when we were born from above – we were like a little baby in need of maturity. James teaches us that maturity is the goal for every Christian. And the mark of maturity is wisdom.

So what is wisdom? Wisdom is experiential or applied knowledge (cf. Prov 1:1-6). It involves intelligence and moral integrity (cf. Prov 8:7-9) as well as expertise and discipline in all areas of life! Wisdom's result is "skilled living." So by asking for wisdom, we are asking for God to give us the ability to navigate through trials with skill. This skill results in actions that are right and pleasing to God. As we endure various trials, we will increase in wisdom and hence become more mature.

Now we were not endowed with all wisdom at our new birth, quite the contrary. As believers, we must grow in wisdom. As we face new and different challenges in our Christian life, we need more and more wisdom. So James reveals a God of wisdom who is ready to give wisdom to His children. James declares God is benevolent, ready to bountifully supply wisdom to His needy children. Even though God is full of wisdom, He in no way looks down upon those who lack wisdom. He will by no means scorn those who ask for wisdom. Those who feel inadequate can rest assured our gracious and loving Lord is thrilled to give wisdom to those who seek it. We must realize how contextually, James is saying God will supply the wisdom for us to successfully endure each and every trial. The condition for obtaining this wisdom is asking! Ask and you will receive (cf. Matt 7:7; Luke 11:9).

By asking, James means we approach God, believing not only that He has wisdom, **but also believing He will impart His wisdom to us!** It is one thing to believe God has wisdom; it is quite another to believe He will give it to us! This stipulation of faith is important to recognize. Those who ask but do not believe that God will give, will not receive anything (1:7).

So what is faith? Faith is the inward conviction that something is true. If we believe something is true, we have been persuaded. Thus, faith is persuasion that something is true. Biblical faith is simply receiving the testimony of God. The opposite of faith is doubt. Hence, when I have faith in what God says, doubt does not exist. If any doubt exists, then I cannot say I have faith (cf. Matt 14:31; 21:21; 28:17; Mark 11:23; Rom 14:23).

Our Christian life began by receiving the testimony of God concerning the gift of eternal life (cf. John 3:16; 5:24; 6:47)! The moment we were confident God was willing and able to give us eternal life, we can say we believed His promise. At this moment of belief we received the promise of eternal life (John 3:18, 36). The promise we see in James concerning wisdom for the trials of life works in a similar manner. The moment we are convinced God has and will give us wisdom, we are then able to receive it. How then will the wisdom arrive? Through a bolt of "wisdom lightening?" No, it actually will come through the trial itself. God will give us wisdom as we by faith walk through the trial, trusting in His provision and deliverance.

How foolish it is for us to doubt God and His provision and care for us! James likens the doubting Christian to a double minded and unstable person. Any of us who doubt the revealed will of God should be advised of our utter foolishness. Our Christian lives will be characterized as defeated and unstable. Instead of doubting God, we must simply believe what He says (of course we must know what He says in order to believe)! Those who trust the Lord are sure and stable, ready to withstand the test (cf. Ps 1:1-3).

James also reminds us the rich as well as the poor brother must rely upon the Lord. The life we have on earth is but a vapor (cf. 4:14). Our focus should be on the quality of life out ahead. The goal for our lives on earth is not to have an easy existence. Rather, it is to traverse through the difficulties with wisdom, grace, and endurance. God has promised to make it worth our while if we seek Him without exalting ourselves. In fact, He has promised to exalt us if we humble ourselves (4:10)! What a promise!

DISCUSSION QUESTIONS AND IDEAS

- What are some examples of wisdom you see in yourself and others?
- Will the wise thing to do always be the popular thing to do?
- Give an example of faith and doubt contrasted.
- Give an example of how you gained wisdom through a trial.

Perseverance Pays

CHAPTER 3
EVIL, SIN, AND DEATH

James 1:13-16

^{13}Let no man say when he is tempted, I am tempted of God: for God cannot be tempted with evil, neither tempteth he any man: ^{14}But every man is tempted, when he is drawn away of his own lust, and enticed. ^{15}Then when lust hath conceived, it bringeth forth sin: and sin, when it is finished, bringeth forth death. ^{16}Do not err, my beloved brethren.

As we think about the subject of evil, sin, and death, we must remember to whom James is speaking – believers. In v. 2 he addresses his readers as *my brethren*. Again in v. 16 he calls them *my beloved brethren* while yet again in v. 19 he refers to them as *my beloved brethren*. The readers are loved by James for they are his brothers and sisters in Christ. Like Paul, James was very concerned with proper understanding or knowledge (cf. Eph 1:15-18). He did not want his brothers and sisters in Christ to be in error. He wanted them to have proper doctrine which would in turn lead to proper living!

Being God's children, we have been given the gift of everlasting life freely (cf. John 3:16; 10:28-29; Rom 5:15)! What a blessing! God in His Omni-benevolence has freely given everlasting life to us. However, we must realize that just because we possess the gift of everlasting life does not mean we cannot or will not be tempted to sin. James now moves to warn us how temptation to sin is a very real threat. He wants us to realize and expect temptation.

First, James tells us we should never accuse or blame God for tempting us. Remember, we must know the truth and not be in error concerning temptation. According to James, God does not tempt us. God does not know how to tempt us for He cannot be tempted with evil – His very nature has no concept of evil or sin (1 John 1:5)! God can only do, participate in, and lead us into what is good. Hence, in the Lord's Prayer, we are instructed to request deliverance from evil (Matt 6:13).

Second, James reveals that because of our own sinful nature, we can be tempted. Look at what James says about temptation – does he say the Devil tempts us? NO! James tells us we are to blame for following temptation. Our own lust pulls us down the path to sin. While the Devil certainly has great power and influence over us (cf. 1 Thes 2:18), we alone are to blame for succumbing to temptation. Satan has the ability to put circumstances in our path allowing us to be tempted, but He does not actually tempt us. So, temptation does not come from God or the Devil. It comes from within our depraved nature. We are drawn away and enticed to sin because we are sinners by our very nature.

At this point it is important to distinguish between a *trial* and a *temptation*. A *trial* is a difficulty or testing we face. In the context of James 1:2-4, a *trial* is something causing us to suffer for Christ – usually some form of religious persecution (being ridiculed for praying; mocked for being modest; accused of wrong because of our allegiance to the Lamb). We should dignify *trials* welcoming them in our lives (cf. Matt 5:11-12)! *Temptation* however is not a trial. A *trial* is allowed by God and many times ordained of God (cf. Job 1 & 2). *Temptation* is something God wants us to flee. *Temptation* is something we allow as we flirt with sin. *Temptation* originates in us; *trials* originate outside us. Again, remember the plea to be delivered from evil in the Lord's Prayer! We are to avoid *temptation*. We are not to make *provision for the flesh* (Rom 13:14). Avoiding *temptation* is accomplished by drawing nigh to God and praying for deliverance (4:7-8; 5:16). It is far better to avoid *temptation* altogether rather than to have to flee *temptation* just prior to sin. If we allow ourselves to be tempted, the likelihood of sin is great.

Notice the process of temptation James outlines. First, a suggestion (maybe an invitation to be where we know we should not be) that we know is not wise. Next, temptation (maybe to drink, participate in lewd behavior, or have a "good time") grips us as we begin to allow the suggestion to take root in our mind. Next, sin (actually participating in what is clearly wrong: hate, jealousy, sexual fantasy, etc.) occurs as we disobey the Lord – sin is an act of our will. Lastly, death (death essentially means separation) results because of sin.

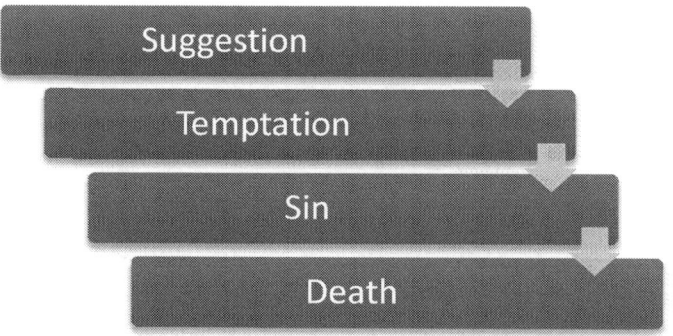

Suggestions to sin come from three basic influences: the world, flesh, and Devil. While none of these actually tempt us, they all provide the environment for temptation. There is no way for any of us to escape the suggestions to sin. However, there is a way to avoid temptation – to walk in the Spirit denying the lust of the flesh (cf. Gal 5:16). The overcoming Christian will be marked by a life of self discipline (cf. 1 Cor 9:27). **There is no shortcut to being victorious in our Christian life.** We must prevail in prayer by seeking the Lord continually (cf. 4:7-8; Matt 26:41). The enemies surround us, but thank the Lord for His provision! He has equipped us with the ammunition to win the battle! We can persevere and be victorious!

The result of sin is death in one form or another. We know the sin of Adam resulted in the most devastating form of death – spiritual death (everlasting separation from God in the lake of fire) for all mankind. Only those who believe on the Lord Jesus Christ can escape this doom of sin. Jesus paid the sin debt for all mankind – those who believe in Him receive the gift of everlasting life, thus escaping everlasting death (cf. Rom 5).

While James is focusing on the effect of sin which results in death, he is not specifically speaking of spiritual death. Death in Scripture can also refer to physical death, psychological death, even social death. James, speaking to believers, shows them the danger of sin – death in its various forms. James is showing how a Christian who sins produces dead works. He does this by contrasting death with life (but not everlasting death and life). Paul uses these terms in a similar manner in Romans 8:6-13. James tells the overcoming Christian how his endurance will result in life – *the crown of life* (1:12). The idea James is conveying is that of abundant life! Conversely, he is telling the defeated

Christian how his sin results in death – the absence of *the crown of life*. Christians cannot be enslaved to sin yet expect to receive the *crown of life* as a reward. Allowing sin to enslave us keeps us from enjoying abundant life in the present as well as in eternity. If our Christian life is characterized by sin, then our dead works will all be burned up at the Judgment Seat of Christ (cf. 1 Cor 3:15). Our gift of everlasting life cannot be lost; but our everlasting reward can be lost. James' analogy shows how a godly outlook in a life of patient endurance results in reward (abundance of life; cf. John 10:10b) while a downward progression into sin results in separation from reward (death). Paul makes a similar point in Romans 8:6-13. As Christians, we have been called to walk in good works (cf. Eph 2:10); but if we walk contrary to God's calling, we will reap what we sow (cf. Gal 6:7: Col 3:23-25; 2 Cor 5:9-11). Both Paul and James want believers to experience abundant life while shunning sin and its various forms of death.

Maybe we are thinking about specific temptations in our lives and the fact that we are in sin or have already sinned. Praise God, we can confess our sin, and God will forgive (cf. 1 John 1:9)! We do not have to live a defeated life characterized by sin! God does not want us to live this way (cf. Rom 6). God does not want us to be controlled by our old nature. Paul said, *Let not sin therefore reign in your mortal body, that ye should obey it in the lusts thereof* (Rom 6:12). Christians can and do sin, but we can re-establish fellowship with the Lord by confessing our sin. As we confess we should turn from our sin to seek the Lord. Repentance from sin will bring us life full of joy. Turning to the Lord and away from our sinful practice will lift the load of guilt thus allowing us to be pleasing to our Lord. Our conscience can be cleansed while freedom to worship in spirit and truth will prevail. Because of our

Lord's grace and mercy, we can escape the consequences of sin and receive the *crown of life*. The Lord wants every believer to receive this reward for enduring trials while avoiding temptation and sin. James wanted us to be "in the know" while avoiding the error of ignorance. He greatly desires us to be wise and faithful – doers of the Word! He wants us to know Perseverance Pays!

DISCUSSION QUESTIONS AND IDEAS

- Give an example of a trial.
- Give an example(s) of temptation.
- Discuss how temptation to sin can result from a trial. Example: a bad attitude can develop because of religious persecution.
- Discuss how to deal with temptation.
- Give an example of how to avoid temptation altogether, i.e. how to make wise choices.
- Tell why you make it a point to avoid temptation so that you please the Lord and anticipate the *crown of life.*

Perseverance Pays

CHAPTER 4
GOOD GIFTS FROM ABOVE

James 1:17-18

¹⁷ Every good gift and every perfect gift is from above, and cometh down from the Father of lights, with whom is no variableness, neither shadow of turning. ¹⁸ Of his own will begat he us with the word of truth, that we should be a kind of firstfruits of his creatures.

The thought concerning temptation and evil which began in verse 13 is concluded in verse 18. James reveals God is good, and He is unable to do anything evil! John tells us God is love – it is at the very core of who He is (1 John 4:8)! Love is fundamental to God's make-up. Love is one of the key attributes of God while another is holiness (1 Pet 1:16). Essentially, God is loving and holy with all of His other attributes complimenting these two. When Jesus became a man, He relinquished some of His prerogatives and privileges (cf. Phil 2:5-8); but He did not cease to be loving and holy nor did He lose any of His attributes of deity. Because of His unchangeable nature, it was impossible for Jesus to be anything but gracious and righteous – loving and holy.

The psalmist said to *worship the Lord in the beauty of holiness.* (Ps 29:2) James concludes his discussion on evil by showing us we have a beautiful Father who loves and gives. What a stark contrast to the image of evil, sin, and death presented in verses 13-15! Sin hates and takes. God is light and life! God is good, and He never can nor will change! He is the same *yesterday, and today, and forever*. (Heb 13:8) Everything He does is with purpose and is perfect or complete. The gift of His Son was the ultimate gift of perfection – for in Him dwells the fullness of God! (cf. Col 1:19) His gift of everlasting life, which He willingly and freely gave to us, is good and perfect.

God alone is able to provide gifts which are both good and perfect. By good and perfect, James means the gifts of God are without sin. Goodness, kindness, and helpfulness describe the flawless gifts of God. The gifts of the Spirit (cf. 1 Cor 12) are thus good and perfect [flawless]. As members of the body of Christ, we have been given gifts from above with which we are to serve one another. By serving one another, we imitate Christ showing forth the goodness and loving-kindness of God.

When God sent His Son to dwell among us, Jesus ministered goodness. The Creator actually came and served the created. He who was without sin became sin (cf. Gal 3:13; 2 Cor 5:21) so that the fallen creation could be restored. The gift of everlasting life is a good and flawless gift freely bestowed by our gracious God. Once given, a gift cannot be taken back, or else it is not a gift. Paul explained this when he said, *the gifts and calling of God are without repentance.* (Rom 11:29) Earlier in Romans Paul referred to the substitutionary death of Christ as being a *free gift* (cf. Rom 5:15-16). Thus, God's *free gift* of eternal life (cf. Rev 22:17) springs from His Omni-benevolence toward all mankind!

James goes on to describe God as the Creator. He is the *Father of lights* – the One who created the heavenly bodies. Being the Creator, He is immutable and unchangeable. While the stars and planets move casting shadows upon each other, not so with the Creator. James uses this description of the Lord and the universe to further show the contrast between virtue and sin – darkness and light. God is light; in Him there is no darkness (1 John 1:5). Satan is the father of darkness (Acts 26:18; Col 1:13) and he is the father of sin (cf. Isa 14:12-17). The Lord is the Father of light and life – His light is life (John 1:4). Hence, good and perfect gifts emanate from above – from the Lord of life.

Knowing God is benevolent and from Him flow good gifts, James emphasizes a specific good gift from above – regeneration. By saying *of His own will begat he us*, James reminds us of our new birth. We have been "brought forth" by God. We have been "birthed" by God. We are children of God – direct creations by the regeneration of our spirit by His Holy Spirit! James, being a great orator, contrasts the birth which results in death with the birth which yields life. Sin gives birth to *death* while God gives birth to us! The word *begat* in v. 18 and the words *bringeth forth* in v. 15 are the same in Greek. James heralds the good news while revealing deep theological truth! God's free gift of eternal life, which comes via the new birth or regeneration, is of His own doing! This gift is truly free and not of our works (past, present, or future). The new birth is a transaction which involves only the work of God, not man (Eph 2:8-9; Titus 3:5). God is the one who calls us *out of darkness into His marvelous light.* (1 Pet 2:9)

Man can in no way "will" himself to have eternal life. God is the giver, and He alone is the one who wills it so. God is life, with all life coming from Him. He and He alone is the giver of eternal life. As we think of eternal salvation from the lake of fire as well as the glorious gift of eternal life we receive from God, we must comprehend that the transaction is all of God's doing. We are passive, and He is active. He offers the free gift, and we simply receive – believe and receive (John 1:12; Eph 2:8-9). Eternal salvation is God's work and not our work! Eternal salvation is a work by Him, for Him, and to Him. In no way is this salvation our work for God; rather it is God's work for us. We can do nothing in mind, action, or attitude to affect the will of God relative to salvation from eternal death. Paul explained God's sovereign decisions when he said:

> [8]Wherein he hath abounded toward us in all wisdom and prudence; [9]Having made known unto us the mystery of **his will**, according to **his good pleasure which he hath purposed in himself:** [10]That in the dispensation of the fullness of times he might gather together in one all things in Christ, both which are in heaven, and which are on earth; even in him: [11]In whom also we have obtained an inheritance, being predestinated **according to the purpose of him** who worketh all things after the counsel of **his own will:** [12]That we **should be to the praise of his glory**, who first trusted in Christ.[Emphasis mine] (Eph 1:8-12)

While Paul elaborates on the will of God relative to mankind, James' short statement sums it up; *of his own will begat he us.* God's will and purpose are supreme, with every other force subordinate. While we should stand in awe at the absolute power and authority of God, we should also bow to worship Him because of His decision to include us in His plan! What a wonderful truth: this awesome God – the Creator of everything –

loves me offering me good and perfect gifts! His most precious gift being the absolutely free gift of eternal life! Hallelujah!

Neither James nor Paul teaches that God has decided to regenerate only a select group of individuals. Quite the contrary, God extends His grace to **all** mankind. Jesus died for the sins of all people (John 1:29; 3:16; 1 John 2:2). It is God's will for every man, woman, teenager, boy, and girl to be saved. Under the inspiration of the Holy Spirit, Paul said so to Timothy:

> [4]Who will have **all men** to be saved, and to come unto the knowledge of the truth. [5]For there is one God, and one mediator between God and men, the man Christ Jesus; [6]Who gave himself a **ransom for all**, to be testified in due time. [Emphasis mine] (1 Tim 2:4-6)

God is good with His mercy and grace extended to all. We should never think Jesus died for a select group of people or a limited number of people. He died for all so He might give them life.

> For God so loved **the world**, that he gave his only begotten Son, **that whosoever believeth** in him should not perish, but have everlasting life. [Emphasis mine] (John 3:16)

The *word of truth* reveals the desire of God that all of mankind be saved – this is His sovereign choice. While God desires all to be regenerated, He does not force any to believe. Mankind can either receive the *word of truth* or reject it (cf. Acts

26:28). Nonetheless, God is at work in the world via the Holy Spirit to persuade men, women, teenagers, boys, and girls (cf. John 12:32; 16:7-11). We do not understand nor can we fully explain the ministry of God to the lost. However, we can take Him at His word. He wants all to be saved and escape the fires of eternal death.

How does God bestow this wonderful gift upon us? How do we know of the wonderful gifts of God? How do we know anything about God or His free gift of eternal life? We know through the *word of truth* (cf. Eph 1:13; Col 1:5; 2 Tim 2:15)! God has declared His will for us to **know** – He has spoken (cf. Heb 1:1-2)! In His great mercy and grace, He has chosen to publish His will (the Bible) so all of humanity might be saved by *His* grace through faith alone (John 1:29; 3:16; 6:47; Eph 2:8-9; 1 Tim 2:4). God has revealed His will to us! He has caused the light of the gospel to shine upon us! When illuminated by this glorious light, we are persuaded by its truth – we believe. Hence, our faith is a passive response to the truth of God. When the *word of truth* is presented to us, we become convicted and convinced that what God says is true (cf. John 16:7-11). God reveals to us our sinful condition and our need for deliverance. This is the work of the Holy Spirit in conjunction with the *word of truth. To believe is to be persuaded that the word of God is in fact true.* Paul described Abraham's faith as being a *persuasion* when he said, *He staggered not at the promise of God through unbelief; but was strong in faith, giving glory to God; and being fully persuaded [convinced] that, what he had promised, he was able also to perform.* [Emphasis mine] (Rom 4:21-22). Later in Romans, Paul declares that faith is possible because of the *word of God* (Rom 10:17). Pause to think for a moment – without the *word of truth* we would not know the will of God! We would be unable to save ourselves or respond in faith for we would not know what to believe. How magnificent is the *word of truth!* As Jesus said, *Thy word is truth.* (John 17:17). Hence, it is imperative we uphold the *word of truth* as the absolute authority. It is not a relative truth; it is absolute truth!

One example of the revelatory nature of God's Word can be observed in Matt 16:17. After Peter's marvelous declaration that Jesus is *the Christ, the Son of the Living God,* Jesus said *flesh and blood hath not revealed it unto you, but my Father which is in heaven.* Peter knew the blessed truth concerning Jesus because the Father wanted him to know – God revealed Himself to Peter. *For God, who commanded the light to shine out of darkness, hath shined in our hearts, to give the light of the knowledge of the glory of God in the face of Jesus Christ.* (2 Cor 4:6) It is God who takes the initiative and action to reveal Himself so we might know His will therefore being regenerated! While we are responsible to seek the Lord (cf. Acts 17:27), we in no way "will" ourselves saved. Rather, we respond to the revealed will of God either by believing or rejecting.

As we continue to absorb the deep theological truth of God's sovereign decision to save all who believe, we should pause to consider another precious truth. God has commissioned us to spread this good news! By being obedient to the Lord, we can partner with Him by declaring His will. How marvelous to think that we can show others our love and God's love by telling them of His plan of salvation! Only when a person hears the good news can they believe it! This is why Paul repeated,

> [14]...how shall they believe in him of whom they have not heard? and how shall they hear without a preacher? [15]And how shall they preach, except they be sent? as it is written, How beautiful are the feet of them that preach the gospel of peace, and bring glad tidings of good things! (Rom 10:14-15)

By referring to preaching, Paul does not necessarily limit the spreading of the good news to a select few "preachers." Rather, he wants all believers to spread the good news to friends, neighbors, fellow students, co-workers, and strangers – everyone!

So why did God birth us? Why did He choose to impart life to us who were dead in sin? In short, because He wanted to! He is love; and because of His loving nature, He made it possible for mankind to escape the consequences of Adam's fall. But, there is more to the story of God's intervention into the fall of mankind. God's glory and sovereignty are the reasons for our salvation. In fact, God's glory is paramount: *Thou art worthy, O Lord, to receive glory and honour and power: for thou hast created all things, and for thy pleasure they are and were created.* (Rev 4:11) God desires for those He has saved by grace through faith to produce good works (cf. Eph 2:8-10). These good works glorify the Lord. Good works flow from obedience bringing honor, glory, and praise to the Lord. The glory of God revealed by the restoration and redemption of mankind is the ultimate reason why God has provided salvation; *that in the ages to come he might shew the exceeding riches of his grace in his kindness toward us through Christ Jesus.* (Eph 2:7) For all eternity the salvation of sinners will be a testimony of God's grace and goodness.

James concludes his thought with an agricultural analogy. When He tells us we are a *kind of first fruits,* he is describing the quality of the harvest. In the Old Testament the first fruits, whether animals or produce, were holy and sanctified to the Lord. By saying we are a kind or type, he is saying we are like what God plans to do for the entire creation. One day God will restore the creation, and it will be "good" just as it was in the beginning (cf. Gen 1). Paul tells us the creation groans waiting for deliverance (cf. Rom 8:19-21). James is saying the gift God has bestowed upon us is but a foretaste of what is to come. In the coming kingdom of our Lord Jesus Christ – referred to as the *regeneration* in Matt 19:28 – only good gifts will come from God! The earth will be rid of the father of sin. As James describes, the gift of life – which comes from above – is but a foretaste and foreshadowing of what is to come. In the *regeneration*, the answer to the great petition, *Thy kingdom come, Thy will be done, in earth as it is in heaven* (Matt 6:10) will be realized. Our present *regeneration* is a type of that which is to come for all creation.

In light of all this awesome theological truth, James gives us very practical advice as we approach each day. We must realize trials and temptations will come. We must not lose sight of our God because He is above the trials! He is able to deliver us from temptation (cf. 1 Cor 10:13)! He is good! He has sovereignly chosen to regenerate us for our good and His glory! We must not blame God for the bad we sometimes experience. Rather, we should rejoice and praise Him for the good gifts He has bestowed. We must not be in error concerning our wonderful loving Lord! He is for us, giving good and flawless gifts. If we are loving Him, He is working in our lives to bring about good (cf. Rom 8:28). He wants to reward us for enduring trials and fleeing temptation.

DISCUSSION QUESTIONS AND IDEAS

- Discuss what it means to be "good" in the context of James.
- Explain how God has given the ultimate "good" gift.
- Discuss the passive nature of faith.
- Ponder the definition of faith being persuasion.
- Discuss and invite questions about good and bad. Some may have questions about their parents' divorce, a friend's death, or a difficult relationship. Show from James that God is good, and He is interested in our well being.
- Talk about having a mindset that looks at the goodness of God, and how proper understanding about God and His goodness should affect our lives.

CHAPTER 5
EARS OPEN – MOUTH SHUT

James 1:19-21

[19] *Wherefore [so then], my beloved brethren, let every man be swift to hear, slow to speak, slow to wrath:* [20] *For the wrath of man worketh not the righteousness of God.* [21] *Wherefore [Therefore] lay apart [put aside] all filthiness and superfluity of naughtiness [overflow of wickedness], and receive with meekness the engrafted [implanted] word, which is able to save [deliver] your souls [lives].*

James' introductory remarks from verses 1-18 have taught us many things. First, believers in Jesus – those who have been born again by the will of God (v. 18) – should expect trials (v. 2). James tells us to not only expect trials, but to also rejoice because of trials. Trials provide us with the opportunity for growth as Christians. He encourages us to persevere through the trials. If we persevere, we are assured of reward – the *crown of life* (v. 12). Hence, there is great motivation to love the Lord – our labor is not in vain (cf. 1 Cor 15:58; Heb 6:10). Second, we have the promise of God's supply of wisdom. For the one who believes Him for wisdom, He benevolently bestows wisdom (v.5-11). Third, we know God is good, and He in no way is evil (v. 13). Fourth, we know temptation, sin, and death result from unwise choices.

James wants us to realize we are responsible for evil and its result (v. 14-16). Fifth, God is the Creator and from Him only flow good gifts. God is the giver of good gifts, and we are simply the recipients. Finally, we know it was God's sovereign choice to make us His children (v. 18). The gift of eternal life was God's choice for He alone has the power to give this gift. God communicated all of His will through His *word of truth*.

With these truths in mind James makes a concluding remark which sets the tone for the remainder of his letter. This is evidenced by the word *wherefore* which could be translated "so then". James in essence is saying: since you know the preceding truths, consider this, your behavior matters! What you say and do is important. It is a life and death issue! Verses 19-20 can be seen as thematic for the entire letter. Our actions as Christians produce either self righteousness which will result in death (not eternal death in James' context) or the righteousness of God which results in life (the *crown of life*). While these truths are applicable to the various situations we encounter, contextually James is referring to how we respond to trials and avoid temptations.

As we look at verse 19, notice to whom James is speaking – His much loved *brethren*. James readily identifies His fellow brethren as those who should heed his instruction and advice. He tells them to do three things: listen well, talk sparingly, and remain under control.

Listen well. James commands believers to be *quick to hear*. It is extremely important that believers listen well to God. God has provided the *word of truth* for various reasons. One is to give us wisdom. The book of proverbs tells us in numerous ways to listen well (cf. Prov 1:8; 2:1; 3:1; 4:1; 5:1). However, our natural tendency is to not listen, especially to instruction in righteous living. Our carnal nature does not want instruction nor does it desire the wisdom from above (3:17).

Paul stressed the need to be instructed by the Word to Timothy in 1 Tim 4:11-16. Throughout his epistles Paul stressed the need to listen and be taught by the *word of truth*. Study Eph 1:15-23; Phil 1:9-11; Col 1:9-10; 2 Tim 2:15 for a taste of Paul's desire for us to have knowledge and wisdom.

Jesus also stressed the need to listen. By listening, He meant we should read, ponder, understand, and know God's Word. On several occasions He said, *He that hath ears to hear, let him hear.* (Matt 11:15; 13:9; Rev 2:7). The point being, it is essential for a Christian to know what God has to say. Without Gods' counsel, we are doomed to fail; only through knowing God's Word can we believe what God has said. Hence, we must be diligent students of the *word of truth*. The lyrics to the song *Word of God Speak*[1] are most inspiring:

> I'm finding myself at a loss for words
> And the funny thing is it's okay
> The last thing I need is to be heard
> But to hear what You would say
> [CHORUS]
> Word of God speak
> Would You pour down like rain
> Washing my eyes to see
> Your majesty

---
[1] Lyrics by Peter Kipley and Bart Marshall.

Perseverance Pays

> To be still and know
> That You're in this place
> Please let me stay and rest
> In Your holiness
> Word of God speak
> I'm finding myself in the midst of You
> Beyond the music, beyond the noise
> All that I need is to be with You
> And in the quiet hear Your voice
> [CHORUS]
> Word of God speak
> Would You pour down like rain
> Washing my eyes to see
> Your majesty
> To be still and know
> That You're in this place
> Please let me stay and rest
> In Your holiness
> Word of God speak
> I'm finding myself at a loss for words
> And the funny thing is it's okay

Talk sparingly. Is this a great piece of advice or what? Actually, no it is a command! It has been well said that God gave us two ears and one mouth! Just based on this fact our ratio of listening to talking should be 2 to 1! We should listen twice as much as we talk. Most of the time, we are eager to spill our guts and complain about the trials we undergo. James is telling us the wise one keeps his mouth shut! Rather than talk, we should remain silent and listen – God may be speaking in the midst of the trial. We cannot learn if we are talking! Yet this is one of the most difficult issues we face – being quiet when under stress. Stress urges us to be vocal and tell everyone how we feel. Psychologists tell us to air our frustrations. Many times we say we just need to "vent." However, James does not prescribe these modern day theories. Rather, he says listen to God and keep your "own wisdom" at bay. God knows all, and our meditation upon Him and His sovereign plan for our life is the answer. He will give wisdom if we in faith ask Him (1:5-11)!

However, James does not say we should never talk. He simply says be hesitant to blab while under stress. After we have listened to the Lord, then we are prepared to speak. Once we have sought the Lord through Biblical meditation and prayer, then we are ready to talk about the trials we face. Wisdom from God's Word should be the primary thing that fills our minds. Only by keeping our mouths shut and ears open can we find wisdom to combat the trial.

Remain under control. When difficulty arises in our lives, our natural tendency is to become angry. We begin to look for the reason for our anger. Usually we find a person(s) to blame. Anger or wrath which is out of control is not wise. The wisdom literature[2] illustrates the need for us to do just as James commands. Proverbs tells us, *He that is slow to anger is better than the mighty; and he that ruleth his spirit than he that taketh a city.* (Pro 16:32) Like the Lord who *is merciful and gracious, slow to anger, and plenteous in mercy* (Ps 103:8), we should seek to control our emotions. But how do we control our emotions?

---

[2] Job, Psalms, Proverbs, Ecclesiastes, and Song of Solomon comprise the Biblical Wisdom Genre.

How do we emulate the Lord who is gracious and patient? How do we exercise patience and kindness? In short, we must be filled with the Spirit (cf. Eph 5:18-21)! In order to be filled with the Spirit we must listen to what He says – we must be filled with the Word (cf. Col 3:16).

Being filled with the Word is paramount. As we meditate upon the Word we will quickly find it demands our action. We are to *put off the old man* and *put on the new man* (Eph 4:22-24). If anger is a problem we face, we must be proactive and diligent to control our anger. Following is a formula for breaking the cycle of uncontrolled anger:

1. Acknowledge your uncontrolled anger as sin (Col 3:8). Uncontrolled anger and wrath are sinful and God tells us to stop sinning in this way. When we face sin head on calling it what it is – SIN – then we have taken a major step. Admitting we have a problem shows we are wise and heeding God's Word.
2. Confess your sin (1 John 1:9). God longs to forgive your sin and restore you to fellowship. Confession is contrary to what our flesh wants, but it allows us to humble ourselves before God. When we humble ourselves, God is able to work mightily in our lives (cf. James 4:8-11).
3. Ask God to help you break the habit of anger (1 John 5:14-15). God will help you if you seek Him earnestly. You will need to be serious and diligent about overcoming your anger. Your emotions are wounded because of sin. You may need to forgive someone for something in order to let go of your anger. You may need to forgive yourself! Many

times we are angry at someone; we need to forgive them, even if they are wrong. God can help us if we want help.
4. Ask God to fill you with the Spirit (Luke 11:13). God's desire is for you to be filled with His Spirit. Ask Him to fill you as you meditate upon His Word. Make it a goal to read Psalm 119. It is divided into 8 verse sections. Meditate upon 8 verses each day, and glean from this awesome Psalm. Look at what the Psalmist is saying, and apply it to your situation. Make some personal comments/notes on each verse. Ask God to fill you with wisdom. The Spirit of the Lord is the Spirit of wisdom. Seek Godly counsel and instruction in the Word. Make it your mission to be a lifelong student of God's Word! If you do, you can be filled with His Spirit!
5. Give thanks for the things that make you angry (1 Thes 5:18). This may sound strange, but it is Biblical. God allows trials and difficulties in our lives to help mold us into better people. Ultimately, His goal is to conform us so that we are just like His Son. Review James 1:1-12 for more insight into this truth.
6. Repeat this formula every time you get angry. You will not simply stop being angry immediately. You will need to be filled with the Spirit on a daily basis. If you get angry and sin, repeating this formula will greatly aid you in breaking the habit of sin. It will remind you of your utter dependency upon God for help. Call upon your Great High Priest – The Lord Jesus Christ – and He will help you in your time of need! (Heb 4:14-16)

In verse 20 James elaborates on the fruit of wrath. It does not produce the type of righteous behavior God expects and in fact demands from His children. Because we have been born again by the *word of truth,* we are now able to live lives pleasing to God. We have been justified and are positionally "righteous." James points out how we should live who we are. In other words, since we are positionally righteous in Christ, we should practice righteousness in our everyday lives. We should live holy and righteous lives reflective of our positional standing in our Lord Jesus Christ. Paul elaborated on this truth by saying,

> [1]What shall we say then? Shall we continue in sin, that grace may abound? [2]God forbid. How shall we, that are dead to sin, live any longer therein? [3]Know ye not, that so many of us as were baptized into Jesus Christ were baptized into his death? [4]Therefore we are buried with him by baptism into death: that like as Christ was raised up from the dead by the glory of the Father, even so **we also should walk in newness of life**. [5]For if we have been planted together in the likeness of his death, we shall be also in the likeness of his resurrection: [6]Knowing this, that our old man is crucified with him, that the body of sin might be destroyed, that henceforth we should not serve sin. [7]For he that is dead is freed from sin. [8]Now if we be dead with Christ, we believe that we shall also live with him: [9]Knowing that Christ being raised from the dead dieth no more; death hath no more dominion over him. [10]For in that he died, he died unto sin once:

> but in that he liveth, he liveth unto God. ⁱⁱLikewise **reckon** ye also yourselves to be dead indeed unto sin, but alive unto God through Jesus Christ our Lord. ¹²Let not sin therefore reign in your mortal body, that ye should obey it in the lusts thereof. ¹³Neither yield ye your members as instruments of **unrighteousness** unto sin: but yield yourselves unto God, as those that are alive from the dead, and your members as instruments of **righteousness** unto God. [Emphasis mine] (Rom 6:1-13)

Verse 21 begins a most important section in James' letter. The word *wherefore,* which could also be translated *therefore,* marks the new section. He has laid the foundation in the first 20 verses. In verses 19-20, James summarizes his main thought for the entire epistle. Beginning in verse 21 he begins to develop the theme put forth in verses 19-20.

Remember, the goal James discusses for the Christian – the *crown of life*! He reminds us that our motivation to endure trials and refuse to sin is love for the Lord as well as reward from the Lord. The hope for reward is a key motivational teaching put forth in Scripture. God has designed mankind to seek excellence, be creative, and achieve greatness. Hebrews Chapter 2 confirms man is destined for regal greatness. Like Paul, James knew our Lord is gracious and loving, wanting to say to us *well done*. According to Paul and James, a crown awaits the faithful which is to be highly sought after:

> ²⁴Know ye not that they which run in a race run all, but one receiveth the prize? So run, that ye may

obtain. ²⁵And every man that striveth for the mastery is temperate in all things. Now they do it to obtain a corruptible crown; but we an incorruptible. ²⁶ I therefore so run, not as uncertainly; so fight I, not as one that beateth the air: ²⁷But I keep under my body, and bring it into subjection: lest that by any means, when I have preached to others, I myself should be a castaway. (1 Cor 9:24-27)

For Paul, attaining the crown was his life's passion! He saw it as his most important achievement. Also, see Phil 3:11-14 as it relates to Paul's greatest desired achievement.

Since James and Paul both recognized the great importance of winning the crown, shouldn't we? Of course! This is the primary reason James writes to us – to show us the reward which results from a life of perseverance! So how do we persevere! How do we live a life pleasing to the Lord? We must lay aside all of our sinful ways! In order to "hear" well, we must first clean out our spiritual ears. Sin many times clogs up our spiritual ears. It must be cleaned out. We must *lay apart* or put aside all filthiness and overflowing wickedness. In Greek, the words *lay apart* carry the idea of removing clothing. James is telling us to take off the dirty sinful clothes so that we might be robed with clean righteous clothing (cf. Rev 19:8). The phrase *superfluity of naughtiness,* which can be translated *overflow of wickedness,* carries the idea that sin is like an abnormal growth – a tumor. Sin is abnormal for a Christian and should be removed just like a tumor should be from a body. If we are going to endure trials and temptations while pressing for the prize of the *crown of life*, we must renounce all sin in our lives. Remember Paul's instruction in Romans 6, we are dead to sin but alive in Christ, therefore we should walk in newness of life. We do this by calling sin just what it is – SIN! Renounce it and lay it aside! (Cf. Heb 12:1-3)

James gives us great practical advice. We who have been *brought forth by the word of truth* (v. 18) should allow that same Word to continue to change us. James tells us the w*ord of truth* has been *engrafted* or *implanted* within us. He likens God's Word to a seed planted within us. It must be nourished in order to produce the desired result. How are we to see the desired result of growth? By receiving the Word with meekness! Meekness is contrasted with the haughty, angry spirit in verse 20 that produces sin and death in our lives. When we receive God's implanted Word with meekness it will change our lives. James even says it will save our soul!

The word for *soul* in Greek is the word *psuche* which can be translated "soul" or "life." While believing the w*ord of truth* can and most assuredly does save from eternal death in the lake of fire, this is not James' meaning in this verse. He is speaking to Christians who have already experienced salvation or deliverance from the lake of fire the moment they believed the gospel (cf. v.18). Instead, James is saying this same Word is able to deliver us in this life to victory. It is able to give us victory over trials and temptations which results in the *crown of life*. Paul spoke of the power of the Word to save in like manner when he said to Timothy,

> [13]Till I come, **give attendance** to **reading**, to **exhortation**, to **doctrine**. [14]Neglect not the gift

that is in thee, which was given thee by prophecy, with the laying on of the hands of the presbytery. **¹⁵Meditate** upon these things; give thyself **wholly** to them; **that thy profiting may appear to all.** **¹⁶Take heed** unto thyself, and unto the **doctrine; continue in them**: for in doing this thou shalt both **save** thyself, and them that **hear** thee [Emphasis mine]. (1 Tim 4:13-16)

Like James, Paul knew the power of the Word of God to save Christians from all of life's calamities. What delivers us from doubt and despair, trouble and trial, sin and death? God does through His precious Word! The psalmist David said,

I sought the Lord, and He heard me, and delivered me from all my fears ... This poor man cried, and the LORD heard him, and saved him out of all his troubles. (Ps 34:4, 6)

The Word of God is able to save us in every respect. The power and potential of this engrafted or implanted Word is enormous! Paul told the Ephesian church, *And now,* **brethren,** *I commend you to* **God,** *and to the* **word of his grace, which is able to build you up,** *and to* **give you an inheritance** *among all them which are sanctified* [Emphasis mine]. (Acts 20:32) Receiving with meekness the awesome gift of God's Word will most assuredly produce change in our lives. This change will result in the most wondrous prize we can ever imagine – a crown! Heed James' strategic advice: listen to God's Word, it will save you!

DISCUSSION QUESTIONS AND IDEAS

- Discuss what it means to listen to God. Quote Ps 4:4 or 46:10.
- Discuss the importance of your fellowship with the Lord. Evaluate your routine of planned time with the Lord.
- Discuss how you have observed the negative effects of anger in yourself or others.
- Discuss the reason for uncontrolled anger/wrath and the way to overcome it.
- Give an example of something you put aside (a sin or distraction from God) that allowed you to walk closer and experience greater fellowship with the Lord.
- Ask for examples of how anyone has been delivered from a great problem via God's Word. Maybe someone has overcome addiction; been set free from habitual lying; restored to their parents or friends.

Perseverance Pays

CHAPTER 6
HEARING AND DOING

James 1:22-25

²²But be ye doers of the word, and not hearers only, deceiving your own selves. ²³For if any be a hearer of the word, and not a doer, he is like unto a man beholding his natural face in a glass [mirror]: ²⁴For he beholdeth himself, and goeth his way, and straightway forgetteth what manner of man he was. ²⁵But whoso looketh into the perfect law of liberty, and continueth therein, he being not a forgetful hearer, but a doer of the work, this man shall be blessed in his deed.

The introduction of the epistle now being completed, James begins to explain what he means by his thematic statement in verses 19-20. To be *swift to hear* does not simply mean to absorb what a Bible teacher says each week. Unfortunately, many Christians listen on Sunday morning, say amen, maybe even raise their hand and shout. I say "unfortunately" because that is all there is to their Christian lives. Christians can be moral faithful people to a certain extent being thought of as "good Christians." However, God desires a fuller and more meaningful existence for His children. James faithfully expounds upon God's will for His children. He will go on in the next several verses – in fact all the way to the end of Chapter 2 – to explain what it means to be *swift to hear.* While we study these verses, we must remember to whom James is speaking – the beloved brethren.

Obedience to the revealed will of God is the subject of verse 22. One could say this verse is the key to understanding James' letter. Obedience is at the heart of fellowshipping with God. Obedience is critical: it allows us the ability to persevere and achieve the reward God wants to give us (cf. 1:12). As children of God – those who have a **relationship** because of the miracle of the new birth (cf. v.18) – we should seek to stay in constant **fellowship** with our Lord. He saved us from eternal death in the lake of fire so that He might bless us with eternal intimate fellowship (cf. John 10:10b). However, intimate fellowship is not assured because of our new birth. Rather, it requires our work and cooperation. God will not fellowship with us if we are living in sin while neglecting His instruction. Further, God will not reward us by saying "well done" if we have not done well! There is no respect of persons with God. He is not a "good old boy" intending to play favorites with His children at the Judgment Seat of Christ (cf. 2 Cor 5:8-11; Col 3:23-25). This is precisely the point of James' letter – obedience will result in blessing while disobedience will result in judgment! We should make no mistakes nor be deceived. Paul made a similar point by saying,

> Be not deceived; God is not mocked: for whatsoever a man soweth, that shall he also reap. For he that soweth to his flesh shall of the flesh reap corruption; but he that soweth to the Spirit shall of the Spirit reap life everlasting. (Gal 6:7-8)

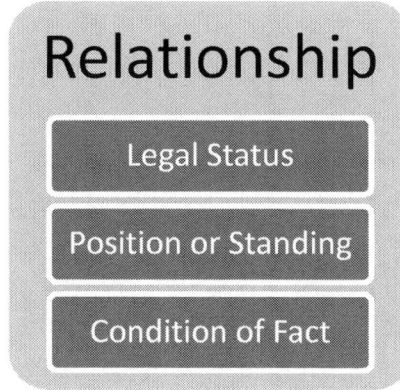 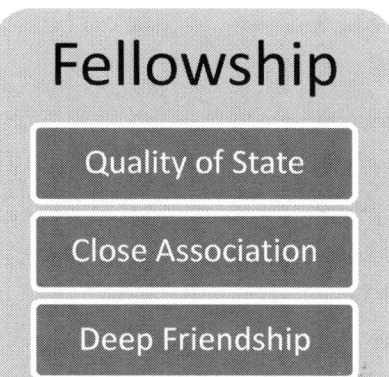

The chart above outlines the difference between a believer's relationship with God versus their ability to have fellowship with Him. Relationship with God refers to our legal status as a child of God (cf. John 1:12). It is a condition of fact referring to our position or standing as one of God's children. Fellowship with God describes intimacy with Him at any particular moment. It refers to the closeness of our walk with Him in time.

Let's take a closer look at what James means by the words *hear* in v. 19 and the word *hearers* in v. 22. The same Greek word is used in both verses. Depending upon context, it can mean to simply listen or understand what has been said or it can mean to listen intently putting what you have heard into practice – to hear responsibly. Hence, to be a hearer only in v. 22 is not to be desired. The one who not only listens but who also incorporates truth into their lives – an obedient hearer – is wise. When we hear God's instruction and then actively begin to incorporate this instruction into our lives, we become wise. Our wisdom can then be said to have come from above (cf. 1:5; 3:17).

Obedience is a major problem we all face. We can believe what God says about a matter, but the next step is to actually do what we know is true and right. Only then can we say we have been *swift to hear* as well as a *doer of the word*. Only then can we be called *wise*.

One modern day example of believing and not doing can be observed by a Christian's prayer life. How many of us believe prayer is powerful? How many believe God answers prayer? How many believe an active consistent prayer life yields power to change our lives and the lives of others (cf. 5:16)? Yet how many are prayer warriors? How many waiver from time to time in their prayer life? Unfortunately, many of us believe a great number of truths, but we are not necessarily obedient. This is where James is so successful at peeling away our Christian masks! He gets down to the nitty gritty. James tells Christians to put their money where their mouth is! James says – just do it!

In verses 23-24 James expounds upon the potential for a child of God to be deceived. He explains how the one who is deceived is like someone who looks in a mirror at himself and shortly thereafter forgets who he really is. What James is saying is since a child of God has been born from above (1:18), he should recognize exactly who he is in Christ – he should understand his legal status as a child of God. The one who looks at himself in the mirror of God's Word and then shortly forgets who he is in Christ is deceiving himself. Instead of forgetting who we are in Christ, we should revel in our position allowing it to greatly influence our daily lives. As noted in our last study, this was Paul's precise point in Romans 6. Other passages encouraging us to live like who we are in Christ are: Eph 4; Col 3; 2 Pet 1:3-11.

Another matter we should consider is the present state of many Christians. It is as if they are sitting in front of the mirror and primping. They think they are really moral and living for God.

They do not drink, smoke, do drugs, etc. While this is certainly the right path to take, God expects more than us reveling in our morality. God wants us to emulate Him – we need to become servants (cf. Matt 20:25-28; John 13). We need to serve the Lord, our brothers and sisters in Christ, and the rest of humanity. Our calling is one of holiness and love. Holiness results in righteous living while love results in compassionate living. God wants us to blend these two aspects of His character into our own lives. We must not be deceived and think that God wants anything less from us!

Knowing God's will regarding our lives is critical. When we realize the importance of obeying the commands of our Lord, we will be changed. We will begin to live full lives characterized by godly wisdom. Notice Jesus' words relative to obedience and wisdom:

> [24] Therefore whosoever heareth these sayings of mine, and doeth them, I will liken him unto a wise man, which built his house upon a rock: [25] And the rain descended, and the floods came, and the winds blew, and beat upon that house; and it fell not: for it was founded upon a rock. (Matt 7:23-24)

Think of how foolish it is to deny the power which is ours! Remember, prior to our new birth we were unable to please God or choose to live righteous lives. However, because of our regeneration by the *word of truth*, each day we can choose who we will serve. God has given us the Spirit of life to change us into what He desires. We have the *implanted word* which is able to grow and produce beautiful fruit in our lives. How dangerous for us to deny this power and walk contrary to the Lord. James over and again will emphasize how important obedience is. He will tell us how being an obedient believer will produce living fruit in our lives. He will tell us obedience will produce a faith which is alive and fruitful as opposed to a faith which is dead and useless.

We should not forget the context of James' statement. He has outlined a less than glorious earthly temporal life for believers. He has told us to expect trials and temptations. James' initial readers were scattered abroad away from their homeland, and living under persecution – they were suffering. Suffering is God's way of bringing about greatness in us. Whether it be physical, emotional, or spiritual suffering, God is at work in our lives; but it is not easy. However, we must not forget our predecessor – the Lord Jesus Christ – of whom it is said,

> [8] Though he were a Son, yet learned he obedience by the things which he suffered; [9] And being made perfect, he became the author of eternal salvation unto all them that obey him. (Heb 5:8-9)

There was no shortcut for Jesus relative to being exalted. In order for Him to achieve His exalted position He was required to suffer (cf. Phil 2:5-11; Heb 2:10; 12:1-3). Just as it was for Him, so shall it be for us. We must listen, love, and obey no matter where that path takes us. We must take up our cross daily and persevere in order to win the *crown of life* (cf. 1:12). Jesus made this very point at the beginning of His Sermon on the Mount. Disciples of the Lord Jesus Christ should expect suffering and trial, but they should also rejoice for great is their reward (cf. Matt 5:1-

12)! This Biblical principle is summarized in the phrase "no cross, no crown!"

Following James in verse 25, we see he now tells us how to be blessed. If we want blessing, we must obey. Of course, in order to obey we must know God's instruction. James identifies God's Word as the *perfect law of liberty*. As we are in God's Word seeking Him and listening to the wisdom He imparts, we can be doers of the Word. Because of our new nature, we can produce deeds which are righteous – it is quite possible! James is introducing the idea that a person who has been born from above can and should produce righteous works in their lives. *Practical righteousness* (the practice of righteous works by a Christian) is only possible from someone who is *positionally* righteous (one who has been declared righteous by God as a result of faith alone in Christ alone). Hence, anyone who is justified *positionally* should strive to be justified *practically*. James is telling us our works count for something. They do not save us from eternal death. They do not earn us our way into heaven. Rather they are pleasing to God allowing us to enjoy His eternal blessing and favor. James will elaborate extensively on *practical* justification or righteousness via works all the way through the end of Chapter 2.

One problem existing among many today is theological. While the average Christian does not think of himself as a theologian, in reality all of us are theologians. What we believe affects how we live. The theological error of many is this: "I do not need to do anything for God because He did it all for me." While some of this statement is true, that does not make it all true. Without doubt God has done what we could not do. While this is certainly true, we must not be deceived into thinking we cannot or should not do anything. Also, we must not be deceived into thinking God is directing us, and we have no influence in the matter. James is telling us to do something. Yes, we are to follow the Lord. Yes, we cannot do it alone. But we are to do it! We are to produce good works through the power of the Spirit of God. The chart above explains the synergy involved with our Christian life. Our Christian life is supposed to be in **cooperation** with the Lord – it is designed by Him to be a synergistic effort (cf. Phil 2:12-13). He is to lead primarily through His Word. We are to follow by doing good works (Eph 2:10). God initiates and provides the power and we follow in obedience to His will. If we think any other way, we are in error – theological error.

Realizing the importance of correct theology, we should think further about what James calls the *perfect law of liberty*. The Word of God is perfect (cf. Ps 19:7-14) producing liberty. When we believed upon the Lord Jesus Christ, not only were we immediately delivered from eternal death and given life, we were also promised the ability to experience abundance of life (cf. John 10:10b). We were set free from the bondage of sin. Relative to freedom, John recorded,

> [31]Then said Jesus to those Jews which believed on him, If ye continue in my word, then are ye my

disciples indeed; [32]And ye shall know the truth, and the truth shall make you free. (John 8:31-32)

God's Word has the power to set us free indeed. God's Word is the absolute authority for all matters of faith and life. Jesus tells those who believe to continue in His Word so they may experience the liberty it can produce. Knowing the truth will set us free in mind and will. Knowing absolute authority allows us to walk in the glorious light of God's will!

As Christians, we should gaze into the mirror of God's Word and examine ourselves. It will encourage, reprove, rebuke, and instruct us. However, we should not look into this mirror introspectively. By introspectively I mean to continually test to see if we have a relationship with God. Introspection will produce doubt and fear. On the other hand, self examination will produce hope and encouragement. Introspection is subjective and based upon our own view of things. Many are introspective struggling with the reality of the new birth in their lives – they are not absolutely sure they have eternal life. Many times they doubt God's promise and look to their own works as proof of their new birth. When they do not measure up, they introspectively look at their lives doubting the reality of their regeneration. This is a vicious cycle. It is not liberty nor is it based on the truth.

Introspection produces a miserable life of fear and discouragement. People should not live this way. Unfortunately, many Bible teachers instruct after this manner. They encourage Christians to look to their works to prove their new birth. The problem with this teaching is that it is subjective. My life may seem righteous today leading me to believe I am saved. But tomorrow it may not. The only way I can know I am saved is to base it upon an objective standard – the *word of truth*! If God has promised eternal life simply upon our belief, then we should base our assurance of salvation only on our belief – not on any of our works! This is precisely what Jesus did with Martha in John 11:25-27. He asked her if she believed His promise, and she said YES! No works of her own – just belief in the promise of the Savior! If you are in doubt, settle this issue once and for all. Believe Jesus' promise of eternal life and receive the gift!

When we look into the *perfect law of liberty* it tells us we are saved from eternal death simply by believing the promise of God (cf. John 3:16; 6:47; Acts 16:31; Eph 2:8-9). It also tells us to obey God's instruction for additional promises and blessing. James is telling us to seek God through His precious Word and stop looking to ourselves. Stop adding to the requirements for the new birth, and put works in their proper place. Examine yourself in the light of God's Word – it will tell you if you are walking in fellowship with Him. It will tell you the proper kind of *work* (1:25) that will result in blessing. Works are important! Thus, James will continue to expound upon them. He will remind us of the teachings of our Lord Jesus Christ. James will tell us the proper kind of *work* a Christian should be doing as well as the benefit for obedience.

DISCUSSION QUESTIONS AND IDEAS

- Discuss the difference between agreeing with God and obeying what He commands.
- Discuss the difficulty of obedience….why is it so hard for us to obey?
- Ask how one can be sure of their salvation from eternal death.
- What is the difference between a relationship with God and fellowship with God?
- Define liberty and freedom. Discuss how living free is so desirable.

CHAPTER 7
PURE RELIGION

James 1:26-27

²⁶ If any man among you seem to be religious, and bridleth [controls] not his tongue, but deceiveth his own heart, this man's religion is vain [useless]. ²⁷ Pure religion and undefiled before God and the Father is this, To visit the fatherless and widows in their affliction, and to keep himself unspotted from the world.

James now mentions what is probably the biggest problem we all have – our *tongue*! He tells us if we do not have control of our mouth, our religion is vain [useless]; quite a statement from the half brother of our Lord Jesus Christ. James goes on to tell us what *pure religion* looks like – how we are to act in our worship and service of the Lord Jesus Christ.

It continues to be of the utmost importance for us to remember the audience to whom James speaks. He is directing his sermon to the *beloved brethren* (cf. 2, 16, 19). He is not questioning whether they are brethren; rather he addresses them as such. He is not saying since your works are sometimes or most times sinful, you are not brethren. Nor is he saying if you do not control your tongue you are going to hell. If he were, this would be quite a depressing epistle. We would be left wondering – am I really born again? Have I been begotten by the *word of truth* or not? **James is not questioning our regeneration based on what we say or do.** He is telling us how to live the Christian life. James knows we are in Christ, so he wants us to act like it! He is telling us how to live out practically what we already are positionally in Christ.

To understand James' point about being *religious* and having *pure religion*, we must think back to the original readers. They were Jewish by natural birth and formerly under the Mosaic system of worship. The Mosaic Law included many outward observable acts of worship and service to the Lord. Remember prayers, fasting, and giving of alms were all part of the Mosaic system. Hence, their religion [a ceremonial worship system] was very observable. If a Jew believed on the Lord Jesus Christ, they would certainly continue in praying, fasting, and giving. They could continue in all these types of *religious* exercises or practices and appear quite *religious*. Imagine the influence of these types of acts especially in the early church. If one had the ability to pray with passion doing so out loud, they could be thought of as being very religious. If they gave great sums of money, they could think to themselves: I am pleasing God by being obedient in giving. They could even fast for several days and think: I have sacrificed for the Lord so He is certainly pleased with me! All of these acts of obedience are good in one sense. However, James is pointing out that in and of themselves, these *religious* practices are not the kind of *religion* God desires.

Religion is not what many think. Having the gift of eternal life is not having *religion* per the Scriptures. We can have eternal life and not be *religious* as James and other Scriptures define *religion*. *Religion* is simply a system of worship and service to God. It is observed by traditions and practices. Paul was quite *religious* as a Jew (cf. Gal 1:13-14), and his zeal was widely known (cf. Phil 3:4-6). As Christians, there is nothing wrong with being *religious*. In fact, we should be *religious* for we exist in order to worship and serve our Lord!

What James is telling us is outward expressions are not all God desires. It is like the Prophet Samuel's proclamation concerning a *religious* act, *And Samuel said, Hath the LORD as great delight in burnt offerings and sacrifices, as in obeying the voice of the LORD? Behold, to obey is better than sacrifice, and to hearken than the fat of rams.* (1 Sam 15:22) While sacrifice is important and in fact commanded, it in and of itself is not what pleases the Lord. Rather, obedience is what the Lord desires. Actually, obedience will result in sacrifice. Obedience reveals the love and devotion one has towards the Lord! God wants to fellowship with us. Being the Creator, it is His prerogative as to how the two of us will fellowship together. This is where our obedience comes into play.

James strikes at the heart of where we live when he zeros in on our tongue. **Control of our mouth is necessary in order to be *religious*.** If we are serving the Lord the way He wants us to serve, we will be kind, merciful, and loving. This type of behavior will be manifested in what we say and how we say it! What is happening in our heart will come out of our mouth! Jesus was quite clear on this point when He said, *A good man out of the good treasure of his heart bringeth forth that which is good; and an evil man out of the evil treasure of his heart bringeth forth that which is evil: for of the abundance of the heart his mouth speaketh.* (Luke 6:45) Jesus, being a student of God's Word, knew the importance of keeping our mouth under control. He knew the Proverbs which say,

"¹³ Righteous lips *are* the delight of kings; and they love him that speaketh right. ¹⁴ The wrath of a king *is as* messengers of death: but a wise man will pacify it. ¹⁵ In the light of the king's countenance *is* life; and his favour *is* as a cloud of the latter rain. ¹⁶ How much better *is it* to get wisdom than gold! and to get understanding rather to be chosen than silver! ¹⁷ The highway of the upright *is* to depart from evil: he that keepeth his way preserveth his soul. ¹⁸ Pride *goeth* before destruction, and an haughty spirit before a fall. ¹⁹ Better *it is to be* of an humble spirit with the lowly, than to divide the spoil with the proud. ²⁰ He that handleth a matter wisely shall find good: and whoso trusteth in the LORD, happy *is* he. ²¹ The wise in heart shall be called prudent: and the sweetness of the lips increaseth learning. ²² Understanding *is* a wellspring of life unto him that hath it: but the instruction of fools *is* folly. ²³ The heart of the wise teacheth his mouth, and addeth learning to his lips. ²⁴ Pleasant words *are as* an honeycomb, sweet to the soul, and health to the bones.... ¹⁹ A brother offended *is harder to be won* than a strong city: and *their* contentions *are* like the bars of a castle. ²⁰ A man's belly shall be satisfied with the fruit of his mouth; *and* with the increase of his lips shall he be filled. ²¹ Death and life *are* in the power of the tongue: and they that love it shall eat the fruit thereof." (Prov 16:13-24; 18:19-21)

Powerful words from God's book on wisdom! James, Jesus, and the writer of Proverbs all tell us the danger of our tongue. The only way to restrain it is to abide in the Lord. If His Words are continually before us with our meditation on Him, then His abundance will flow from us! This abundance manifested in us will be holiness, mercy, and love. This is *pure religion*!

So, if we are not practicing *pure religion*, then we are deceiving ourselves relative to our religious activities. Again, James is not saying we are void of eternal life. Rather, he tells us our fellowship with God is lacking. When our fellowship with the Lord is lacking, then our mouth will reveal it. Hence, our *religion* will be useless to God. It will be something He is not pleased with nor can He use. Our actions – our *religious* actions – must be done in the context of fellowship with God. We must be on good terms with Him. If we are not in fellowship with the Lord, our *religious* activities are vain, and we are deceived if we think they are not vain. For more study on this subject, consult the book of 1 John and Revelation Chapters 2 and 3. In Rev 2:1-5, Jesus commands the Ephesian believers to repent and fall back in love with Him. This is where we as believers must strive to excel – in the freshness of our love for the One who loved us (and still loves us) when we were unlovable!

As Christians, if we find ourselves in this situation how can we change? How can we remedy vain religious activities like: cold prayers, heartless singing, grudgeful giving, and spiteful service? By first confessing our sin to God and repenting of our sinful ways. This will bring restoration to our fellowship with God (cf. 1 John 1:9). We must then become students of the Word and what better place to start than with the book of James!

If we want to be *pure* practicing *pure religion* that God accepts, we must abide in the Lord (cf. John 15:1-17; 1 John 2:28)! When we do so, we will be students of God's Word. We will study the life of the Lord Jesus Christ. What did He do on a daily basis? He prayed, fasted, studied/meditated upon the Word, **and served others**! Make no mistake, Jesus was a servant to God and man. In fact, He still is serving as High Priest of the believer (cf. Heb 4:14-16; 7:25)! That is mind blowing! It shows us the character of our Lord. He is a loving, merciful, longsuffering, and giving God! He is everything which is *good* (1:18).

What James discusses theologically, he really addresses practically. He shows us what is in our heart. He does not assume we will please God all the time simply because we are Christians. He knows this is not the case. He shows us how we are in a struggle to practice *pure religion*. It is a struggle against the world, flesh, and devil to serve others out of a love for God which manifests itself in a love for others. Our love should especially be manifested towards those who cannot necessarily love us – the poor and disadvantaged. *Pure religion* is practiced when we serve expecting not to be served (cf. Matt 20:25-28; Luke 6:35-38; John 13:1-17).

Let's think more about *pure religion*. Remember, James has discussed being *doers of the word* (v. 22) as well as being a *doer of the work* (v. 25). His differentiation between *work* and *word* is not a slip of the pen. In verse 27 he incorporates both. If we are a *doer of the work* we will visit and care for those less fortunate. If we are a *doer of the word* we will be morally pure. *Pure religion*, according to James, incorporates both of these actions. In order to worship God on His terms, we must be a loving holy servant – just like Jesus. When we do this, we can expect the same commendation from the Father that Jesus received (cf. Matt 3:17). In fact, this will be the defining moment in our Christian life. Our goal as Christians is to practice *pure religion* so we will hear "well done my son, your reward is the crown of life" (cf. 1:12; Matt 25:23).

It is easier to acknowledge what James says than to put it into practice. It takes **work** to practice *pure religion* that is undefiled. It takes self discipline and reliance upon the Lord. As mentioned earlier in our study, our Christian walk is designed by God to be in cooperation with Him (cf. Phil 2:12-13). He will lead (cf. Rom 8:14), and we are to follow (cf. Eph 5:1). We are to work for the Lord and hence practice *pure religion*. How can we do it? For some it is easier to serve others while their moral character is in question. For some it is easier to be morally pure yet be cold towards the needs of others. However, James reveals that God requires both moral purity with works motivated by love in order to please Him. This is difficult for all of us. We would really rather it be one or the other instead of both! However, we must come back to our perfect example – the Lord Jesus Christ. He was the example we should follow. He was a loving, holy servant of His Father. His words regarding *pure religion* were summed up when He told us to love the Lord and our neighbor (cf. Matt 22:34-40). No matter what, we should love the Lord with our whole being. The same goes for our fellow man…regardless of race, color, culture, hair style, clothing style, etc.

Serving others can be a difficult and uncomfortable chore – especially when viewed through our old nature. However, we are encouraged to lay ourselves on the altar and be renewed in our minds by the Word of God (cf. Rom 12:1-2). We are to die daily to our selfish desires and seek the will of our Father. This means husbands love and seek ways to serve their wives. They should look for ways to encourage their wives in the Lord. It will involve spending time in prayer over their wife asking the Lord to give direction. For wives, it involves the same type of discipline. For children, prayer and seeking the Lord is important. Children have many choices to make and choices made early in life have lasting effects. Choosing to be under subjection to parents is difficult but rewarding (cf. Eph 6:1-3). By serving family members as God outlines in His Word (cf. Col 3:18-25), we enjoy the benefits of God's blessing. However, we must know of God's direction and discipline ourselves according to His plan.

James emphasizes we should seek to worship the Lord *in the beauty of holiness* (cf. Ps 29:2). James tells us to *keep* ourselves. What does it mean to *keep* ourselves? It means to guard ourselves or to be on guard. We must expect opposition – the devil wants us to be entangled with the world and his system (cf. 2 Tim 2:3-5). Jesus told us to *Watch and pray, that ye enter not into temptation: the spirit indeed is willing, but the flesh is weak.* (Matt 26:41) Paul told us, *But put ye on the Lord Jesus Christ, and make not provision for the flesh, to fulfil the lusts thereof.* (Rom 13:14) We are to operate knowing the adversary wants to relieve us of our crown (cf. Rev 3:11). The Devil cannot take eternal life from us, but he can affect our reward. This is his goal relative to Christians. Notice Peter's words on the subject of our adversary,

> [8] Be sober, be vigilant; because your adversary the devil, as a roaring lion, walketh about, seeking whom he may devour: [9] Whom resist stedfast in the faith, knowing that the same afflictions are

accomplished in your brethren that are in the world. ¹⁰ But the God of all grace, who hath called us unto his eternal glory by Christ Jesus, after that ye have suffered a while, make you perfect, stablish, strengthen, settle you. (1 Pet 5:8-10)

Knowing these things, we must be intentional about our *religion*. We must plan to practice *pure undefiled religion*. For if we do not, we will practice dirty, vain *religion* which is not pleasing to or rewarded by God.

Notice the word *and* in the last part of v. 27: *Pure religion and undefiled before God and the Father is this, To visit the fatherless and widows in their affliction, and to keep himself unspotted from the world.* The word *and* is in italics. When the King James translators developed the translation, if there was not a corresponding Greek word, they would generally italicize the English word. The translation could read "To visit the fatherless and widows in their affliction to keep himself unspotted from the world." Do you see what James is saying? If we involve ourselves in the service of others, it enables us to avoid being stained by the world's system! Our loving service actually helps us become as well as stay morally pure. Service to others less fortunate also helps us keep our lives in perspective. Helping others can relieve us of doubt, depression, selfishness, and many other problems associated with our old nature. James gives us a very compact formula for living out our position in Christ. While not exhaustive, James provides very practical advice for how we are to live. Consequently, we are the benefactors when we serve others.

James Chapter 1 concludes with the description of a Christian who is practicing *pure undefiled religion.* This person approaches his daily walk with Christ seriously. He arranges his entire life in such a way that anticipates the battle and subsequent victory! He plans for victory knowing it is imminent – for the Lord is on his side! He undoubtedly faces trials and temptations, but endures via a close walk with the Lord. This walk certainly involves Biblical study and meditation, prayer, fasting, and service to others. What a vivid picture to ponder! What a lifestyle to which we should aspire – one which results in a *crown* (cf. 1:12)!

DISCUSSION QUESTIONS AND IDEAS

- Define religion.
- Discuss how powerful the tongue is and what it reveals about a person.
- Talk about the negative impact of foul language, smart remarks, and hateful overtones.
- Give examples of pure religion in your life or the lives of Christians you admire.
- Give an example of how a person can practice pure undefiled religion.
- Discuss the positive aspects/results of practicing pure undefiled religion.

Perseverance Pays

CHAPTER 8
HONOR WHO – RICH OR POOR

James 2:1-7

^{1}My brethren, have not the faith of our Lord Jesus Christ, the Lord of glory, with respect of persons. ^{2}For if there come unto your assembly a man with a gold ring, in goodly apparel, and there come in also a poor man in vile raiment [filthy clothes]; ^{3}And ye have respect to him that weareth the gay [fine] clothing, and say unto him, Sit thou here in a good place; and say to the poor, Stand thou there, or sit here under my footstool: ^{4}Are ye not then partial in yourselves, and are become judges of evil thoughts? ^{5}Hearken, my beloved brethren, Hath not God chosen the poor of this world rich in faith, and heirs of the kingdom which he hath promised to them that love him? ^{6}But ye have despised the poor. Do not rich men oppress you, and draw you before the judgment seats? ^{7}Do not they blaspheme that worthy name by the which ye are called?

Chapter 2 begins with a plea to the *brethren* – those who have already been born again. We must continue to be cognizant of those to whom James speaks. James continues to expound upon the importance of being *swift to hear*. He gives believers more insight and instruction. Being a *hearer* should translate into being a *doer*. James tells us to put what we believe and teach into practice. In other words, James is saying practice what you preach. Practicing what you preach means we are to practice *pure religion. Pure religion* is holy worship. We learned in the last few verses of Chapter 1 to properly serve God, we must be servants to others. Jesus was the prime example of this kind of worship. Everything Jesus did was pleasing to His Father. Jesus was a man who worshiped God in spirit and truth. James wants us to understand worship and service to God is expressed in very practical ways.

James' words to the brethren are forceful and convicting. He basically tells them to stop being partial. The problem of partiality was a problem 2000 years ago, and it still is today. These believers were respecting people who were considered rich while at the same time debasing those considered poor. Being a respecter of persons is not something God has or ever will practice. James knew the Old Testament attested to the fact God was not at all impressed with the earthly stature of men (cf. Deut 10:17; 2 Chron 19:7; Job 34:19). God is gracious and loving, not casting aside anyone simply because of their race, gender, or financial stature. God offers His **free gift** of eternal life to all men (cf. John 3:16; Rom 5:15; 1 Tim 2:4). Further, God is willing to bless and reward those who love him with things they cannot even imagine – regardless of their temporal earthly status (cf. Matt 19:28-29)!

After the salutation in 1:1, James 2:1 is the first reference to Jesus in the epistle. James, the half brother of Jesus, describes Him as our *Lord Jesus Christ, the Lord of Glory*. James knew all too well of Jesus' Deity, majesty, and power.   James was an eyewitness of the risen Lord Jesus Christ. His readers needed to be reminded that their faith (what they believed) was grounded in the Lord of Glory. God Almighty, robed in human flesh, had come to redeem and restore the fallen creation. It was this great Godman the brethren had trusted. The phrase *the faith* is descriptive of the body of belief or the doctrines they believed. It is much more than a simple belief in the promise of John 3:16. Believing in Jesus for eternal life is the foundation of *the faith*. *The faith* involves all of Jesus' doctrine. It is the body of teaching presented to us in the Scriptures. Paul tells believers to be strong in *the faith* (1 Cor 16:13). This means we are to be mature, continuing to grow in the Lord. Being strong in *the faith* means being diligent to hear and do God's Word. It means to be obedient to the doctrines of our Lord no matter the circumstances, loving the Lord with our innermost being.

Thus, James tells us to practice what we preach by not being partial to others. This is difficult because of our fallen nature. James gives the example of how these believers were treating the rich as opposed to the poor. The rich were being treated with respect and honor while the poor were treated with disdain and shame. This should not be, especially when the brethren meet to worship. However, it happens more than we may like to think. Many times the poor envy the rich, and the rich look down upon the poor. Both rich and poor can be guilty of showing partiality. No matter which class we fall into, we are not immune from partiality.

The picture James paints is of a well dressed, GQ man coming into a meeting of the brethren and being given the best seat in the house. The poor man who comes to the meeting dressed in an ugly, dirty polyester suit is told to stand in the corner. All of this happens because of outward appearance and perceived social status. These believers are guilty of judging a book by its cover. James calls this type of conclusion an *evil thought*. We must always be careful not to judge the worth of any person based on outward appearance. Rather, we must be loving and kind to all. We must make everyone feel welcome and show honor to all. Showing favoritism is very dividing and quenches the Holy Spirit of God. Showing favoritism is wrong because believers have received the grace and mercy of God without cost. We have been given eternal life solely based upon the will of our loving and gracious Father (cf. 1:17-18). Because we are recipients of this type of impartial gift from God, we should emulate our gracious Father. Of note, in James' day the place of meeting was most likely in someone's house, not in a church building.

James next tells the brethren to listen up when he says *hearken*! He wants them to pay close attention, for in acting the way they have been is a gross miscalculation. James reveals a principle – God has chosen the poor to actually be rich. The poor are more inclined to be *rich in faith*. By *rich in faith*, James means deep or abounding in belief. It is one thing to believe in Jesus for eternal life; it is quite another to believe Him for your next meal! Many believers are saved because they exercised a little bit of faith by believing on the Lord Jesus for eternal life. This is the first step towards becoming *rich in faith*. But how much do we trust God for daily provision? Do we believe God can deliver us from evil? If so, why do we not pray more and ask Him to do so? Do we believe God will give wisdom to us? Do we believe God is gracious and wants to reward us for being faithful (cf. 1:12)? We should for He promises us all these things!

It is ironic that God has allowed those who are poor to be *rich in faith*. In fact, James reveals God has chosen the poor for this privilege. God is concerned about the poor: He desires to bless them. The poor were a special focus of Jesus' ministry (cf. Matt 11:5; Luke 4:18). The poor are who God has chosen to be *rich in faith* (cf. 1 Cor 1:26). This election of God is a mystery, but God's ways are not our ways. Some may conclude God does show partiality since He has chosen the poor. While God has chosen the poor, He has not excluded the rich. God is impartial since He offers eternal life to whosoever will. He also offers eternal reward to anyone – rich or poor – who will obey Him and become *rich in faith* (1 Tim 6:5-19).

    The Scripture gives us many examples of those who had exceptional or abundant faith (*rich faith*). Matt 8:10 describes great faith when the centurion tells Jesus all He has to do is speak, and his servant would be healed. Jesus praised him for his great faith. This centurion understood the power of Jesus the Messiah believing His very Word would heal. This was not the case with Jesus' disciples at times (cf. Matt 6:30; 8:26; 17:14-21; Luke 17:6). Other passages which highlight exceptional faith are: Matt 15:28; Acts 6:5; 11:24; Heb 11.

    A point of clarification is necessary on the concept of *great* or *rich faith*. Faith itself means to be convinced something is true. You cannot be 50% or 75% convinced. Faith cannot be measured in fractions. One either believes 100% or not. To have *rich faith* means you believe in spite of numerous obstacles. It means you have been exposed to the facts and are convinced of the promises of God's Word. To have *rich faith* means: you believe God has given you eternal life, He will give you wisdom, He cares for you, and He will reward you for your faithfulness. When we have *rich faith* we believe all these things and more, no matter the circumstances. In order to have *rich faith* we must listen – we must be *swift to hear*!

Again, the ironic thing is that those who are poor are generally better able to trust the Lord. They are many times desperate and more easily persuaded to believe God's promises. This is not to say only the poor can believe or be *rich in faith*. The rich can also have great faith, but there are many obstacles in their path. Paul knew this truth all too well, warning believers about being desirous of earthly riches in 1 Tim 6. In this chapter, Paul addresses both rich and poor telling them not to be deceived by the desire for earthly riches. Paul tells them to lay up riches in heaven just as Jesus commanded (cf. Matt 6:19-20). Consequently, we should evaluate our own status and determine if we are rich or poor. Determining this status is difficult. In many ways every American is rich compared to others in the world. America has the highest standard of living of any country. Within America there are rich, poor, and those in the middle. However, if we take Paul's description of wealth in 1 Tim 6, he seems to say if we have any more than food and clothing, then we can be considered rich. He tells us to be content simply with the basic necessities of life.

James next explains the brethren who are *rich in faith* are *heirs of the kingdom*. He conveys that those *rich in faith* also love God. When Jesus comes again He is going to set up His kingdom (cf. Matt 16:27-28; 19:28-30; 25:30; Rev 11:15; 20:4-6). His kingdom is the focus of the majority of Scripture. In fact, one could say it is the primary theme of Scripture. Earlier James told us those who endured temptation would be rewarded with the *crown of life*. This *crown* is promised to those who love God (cf. 1:12). Notice the connection between being rewarded with a *crown* and being an *heir of the kingdom*. Wealth, nobility, and regality are afforded those who own a *crown* and possess the kingdom. The *crown* given to the faithful believer who loves God will be used by this believer in the kingdom to help King Jesus administer loving justice! The *crown* and ownership in the kingdom is a reward we must visualize by faith. Those who love God will be rewarded with rulership – co-heirship with Christ in His kingdom (cf. Rom 8:17b; Heb 1:9; 14). Hence, co-rulership with Christ in His coming kingdom has been promised to the faithful who love God (cf. 2 Tim 2:12; Rev 2:26-28). James explains to be *rich in faith* and to *love God* go hand in hand. God's desire for every believer is that they be *rich in faith* and receive a *crown* so they can enjoy the privilege of inheritance in His kingdom (cf. Col 3:23-24). This inheritance is of vast worth! The royal status God's faithful will enjoy alongside Christ is beyond imagination. This glorious privilege was certainly in Paul's mind when he said, *Eye hath not seen, nor ear heard, neither have entered into the heart of man, the things which God hath prepared for them that love him.* (1 Cor 2:9)

In verses 6 & 7, James shows the gross error of disregard for the poor. Those who elevate the rich and debase the poor are in direct opposition to God. James goes on to explain that in general, the rich cause harm to believers and blaspheme the Lord of Glory. Again, not all the rich do so, but in general it is true. Hence, in a very down to earth and practical way, James reveals the error of partiality.

Our desire should be to honor all people no matter their status. We are not to show partiality based on this fleeting world's status. We should endeavor to serve others, be rich in faith, love God, and strive to earn the reward He so greatly wants to award us. James tells us to hearken – to listen closely to these truths! Honor God and He will in turn honor you (John 12:26)!

DISCUSSION QUESTIONS AND IDEAS

- Ask for examples of how we can show favoritism.
- Ask or tell of how partiality has affected you.
- Discuss what it means to be poor or rich. Use 1 Timothy 6 as a resource for defining rich or poor.
- Tell a story of how someone you know looks one way, but is quite another.
- Describe what it means to be rich in faith.
- Ask yourself if you are striving to be rich in faith and showing God you love Him. If you are not, why?

CHAPTER 9
THE ROYAL LAW

James 2:8-13

⁸If ye fulfill the royal law according to the scripture, Thou shalt love thy neighbour as thyself, ye do well: ⁹But if ye have respect to persons, ye commit sin, and are convinced of the law as transgressors. ¹⁰For whosoever shall keep the whole law, and yet offend in one point, he is guilty of all. ¹¹For he that said, Do not commit adultery, said also, Do not kill. Now if thou commit no adultery, yet if thou kill, thou art become a transgressor of the law. ¹²So speak ye, and so do, as they that shall be judged by the law of liberty. ¹³For he shall have judgment without mercy, that hath shewed no mercy; and mercy rejoiceth against judgment.

After exposing the sin of partiality in 2:1 and the fact that it backfires anyway in 2:6-7, James now expounds upon the primary teaching concerning relationships. James tells us love is the ultimate realm in which we can and should operate – it is **royal** in nature. He encourages us to consider the Law of Moses and its far reaching ramifications and effects. He also shows us we should be quick to emulate the Lord Jesus Christ by being merciful. When we show mercy, we reap mercy. If we do not show mercy to others, we cannot expect to receive it from the Lord on the day of judgment.

James continues his theme of being *swift to hear* by again quoting Scripture. The command to love others as ourselves is not found for the first time in the New Testament. While some have said the Law of Moses does not show love, this is not the case. Leviticus 19:18 declares, *Thou shalt not avenge, nor bear any grudge against the children of thy people, but thou shalt love thy neighbour as thyself: I am the LORD.* God is love and the law is both holy and loving. God operates in love and holiness. His law reflects both of these attributes.

When Jesus taught, He held a high regard for the Law of Moses. Of course, the Law of Moses was holy and just, revealing God's righteousness and man's sin. Jesus was the one and only man who could completely fulfill the Law of Moses. Jesus battled with the worshipers of the Law of Moses – the Scribes and Pharisees. Once He told them, *But woe unto you, Pharisees! for ye tithe mint and rue and all manner of herbs, and pass over judgment and the love of God: these ought ye to have done, and not to leave the other undone.* (Luke 11:42) The Pharisees had the wrong view – they did not understand the God of the Law! They were interested in the minutia of the Law neglecting to focus on the big picture. They were extremely partial, not interested in fulfilling what James calls the *Royal Law* – LOVE! Love truly is royal! It is delightful to observe how James ties the royal nature of the kingdom with love. The coming kingdom of our Lord Jesus Christ will operate in love (cf. Rom 14:17). James shows that those who love God (2:5) and who love their neighbor (2:8) are truly acting in a *royal* manner. Those who do so will enjoy all the royal benefits of the coming kingdom. As they love others and show mercy, they will reap mercy in the kingdom (cf. Matt 5:7). These overcomers will be crowned with the *crown of life* (cf. 1:12) as kings in the coming kingdom. Their destiny is regal in nature as they will accompany King Jesus in His benevolent reign!

Jesus taught us the most important commandments were to love the Lord and our neighbor (Matt 22:37-40). He said the Law and the Prophets rest upon these two commandments. Thus, to say the Law of Moses does not show love is certainly a misunderstanding of this Law. Jesus gave us the clarity we need to understand that God is love, and we are to imitate Him. All of the New Testament commands us to love the Lord and one another. We cannot have fellowship with one another the way God intends without love. It must be our basis for connecting and interacting with one another.

While it is easy to say we should relate to one another in love, it is not always easy to do so. Our old nature does not operate out of love. Our old nature is selfish, wanting to provide for itself **at the expense of others**. In a very practical way, James hones in on an area in which we all have trouble – partiality. His skillful pen draws from truth about the Law of Moses. James tells us that when we prefer one brother or sister over another based on social status, we are breaking the Law of Moses. He then goes on to tell us the *Royal Law* is also broken. While the Law of Moses has been fulfilled and we are now under grace, this does not mean we are free to be lawless (cf. Gal 5:13-14)! Rather, while under grace we are governed by the Law of Christ which is love. The Law of Christ (John 13:34-35; Gal 5:13-14; 6:2) governs the current dispensation of grace (cf. Eph 3:2). The Law of Christ is the *Royal Law* mentioned by James. The Law of Moses is summarized in the 10 commandments, of which nine are repeated in the New Testament (the observance of the Sabbath is excluded as a law we should observe). Hence, while not under the Law of Moses, we are under the Law of Christ which is actually a higher Law. So we can say when we fulfill the Law of Christ – to love – we also fulfill the Law of Moses.   Nothing is more noble or pleasing to the Regal Ruler of the Universe than for His children to love one another. Love abides forever and is the greatest of Christian virtues according to Paul (cf. 1 Cor 13:13). No wonder James says if we fulfill the *Royal Law* of love we do well!

    Isn't it interesting how many times we want to know God's will for our lives? We get bogged down with the minutia of life wondering what God wants us to do. God's #1 command and will for our lives is that we love Him and others. This takes time and focus on our part. We must study the Scripture and be doers of the Word. We need to revel in the goodness, mercy, and love of God. When we come to Him **daily** in thanksgiving and praise, we will begin to understand how we can love. To love God and others takes time – focused and purposeful, quality time.

    James goes on to speak of judgment for believers. While we who have been born again will never be judged to determine our eternal fate, we will be judged for our works as Christians. James' words are to believers who certainly have a judgment day coming at the Judgment Seat of Christ (cf. Rom 14:10-12; 1 Cor 3:11-15; 2 Cor 5:9-11). His burden is for believers to be victorious in their walk of faith so they can look forward to the *crown of life* (cf. 1:12). To do so requires a walk of faith governed by the highest Christian virtue – LOVE. Love is kind and compassionate. It is merciful, willing to forgive and forget. Love rejoices in the truth, speaking the truth in all situations (cf. 1 Cor 13; Eph 4:15).

    Since we know we will be judged, it would be nice to know the basis upon which our Lord will judge us. James tells believers they will be judged by the *law of Liberty*. The *law of liberty* refers to the Word of God as revealed in the New Testament. Jesus told us He was going to judge His children according to their works (cf. Matt 16:28). He commanded us to be merciful as our Father was merciful. Jesus told us to love as His Father loved (Luke 6:36-37). Both James and Jesus motivate us to love by showing us the benefit we will receive on our judgment day. If we show mercy today, we can expect mercy in that day of judgment. If we do not show mercy today, we cannot expect mercy on that day. The mercy we want on that day is to hear "well done my good and faithful servant." In order to hear this commendation, we must be *swift to hear* – doers of the Word and work. Doing so means we will have fulfilled the *Royal Law* of Love. Fulfilling the *Royal Law* means we have acted like our royal Lord. Thus, in accord with His promise He will then reward us with positions and privileges of royalty alongside His majestic Messiah – the Lord Jesus! What a royal promise!

DISCUSSION QUESTIONS AND IDEAS

- Discuss again what it means to show partiality.
- Ask why it is wrong to show partiality.
- Ask if there are big sins and little sins with regard to the law.
- Discuss the need to show mercy now. Ask if there is an individual benefit in showing mercy.
- Explain the ways we can all become more like the Lord showing love and mercy.

CHAPTER 10
FAITH – ALIVE OR DEAD

James 2:14-20

^{14}What doth it profit [advantage or benefit], my brethren, though a man say he hath faith, and have not works? can faith save [deliver] him? ^{15}If a brother or sister be naked, and destitute of daily food, ^{16}And one of you say unto them, depart in peace, be ye warmed and filled; notwithstanding ye give them not those things which are needful to the body; what doth it profit [advantage or benefit]? ^{17}Even so faith, if it hath not works, is dead [useless], being alone. ^{18}Yea, a man may say, Thou hast faith, and I have works: shew me thy faith without thy works, and I will shew thee my faith by my works. ^{19}Thou believest that there is one God; thou doest well: the devils also believe and tremble. ^{20}But wilt thou know, O vain man, that faith without works is dead [useless]?

Thus far in our study, James has taught us much concerning our daily activities as Christians. He has told us to be hearers as well as doers of the Word. We are to practice what we preach. James has told us to expect trials and allow them to mature us, flee temptation, and rely upon the Lord for wisdom and deliverance. If we do these things, we can expect a reward – the *crown of life*!

The present section is addressed to the *brethren* – those who are already born again. James is asking a question that stems from his command to be hearers and doers. If we are walking with the Lord in intimate fellowship with Him, we will practice *pure religion*. *Pure religion* is true and proper worship which pleases the Lord. We as Christians can and should practice *pure religion*. But what if we do not? This is the issue with which James is dealing.

This *pure religion* emanates from a heart of love. James, reiterating the teaching of Jesus, tells us to make sure we fulfill the *Royal Law* – Love! Knowing we are royal in our position in Christ (we are seated in the heavens together with Christ – Eph 2:6) should affect our daily life while on earth. James has carefully shown his readers how love should be manifested to all men, no matter their social status. He pulls no punches and tells us showing partiality based on social status is a failure to show love and hence is sin (cf. 2:9). By showing partiality, James means the original readers were not welcoming the poor into their fellowship; they were not being friendly and accommodating. According to James, sin of any sort constitutes a breaking of the Law of Moses but more importantly, a breaking of the Law of Christ – the *Royal Law* of love (cf. 2:8-13; John 13:34-35; Gal 5:13-14; 6:2). James has also revealed the royal benefits of loving God and our fellow man – the reward of a *crown of life* and inheritance (ownership) in the coming kingdom of Christ (cf. 1:12; 2:5).

The passage before us (2:14-20) is often misunderstood. It must be appreciated within the context of the book of James. James is addressing the practical actions of Christians. He is instructional as well as critical in how he addresses us. James cares enough to tell us the good and the bad. He truly has a pastor's heart. He is our friend and many times *faithful are the wounds of a friend* (Prov 27:6). James wants us to practice our faith, thus making it alive!

Our faithful friend James asks a rhetorical question in v. 14 which anticipates the answer "no." The issue James raises is our profit (actually the lack of profit) for being a hearer but not a doer. He is dealing with the ramifications of our disobedience to God. James asks if faith without works can save us. Again, based on the grammatical construction in Greek, the answer is no. This answer has haunted many Christians for centuries. It caused Martin Luther to reject the book of James as a part of inspired Scripture. Martin Luther knew salvation from hell was without works. He felt there was no way to reconcile the teaching of James with that of Paul. Paul declared faith – absent of any kind of works – was all that was necessary to save someone from hell (Rom 4:1-8; 5:1; Eph 2:8-9). When asked by the Philippian jailer what he must do to be saved from hell, Paul simply proclaimed, *believe on the Lord Jesus Christ and thou shalt be saved.* (Acts 16:31) Works do not save anyone from hell neither before, during, nor after they believe. Oddly enough, Paul and James use the same person, Abraham, to prove their point about salvation. In Rom 4:1-8, Paul points out the absence of Abraham's works while James emphasizes the presence of Abraham's works in 2:21. We will discuss this issue in our next chapter.

Whether we like it or not, James teaches salvation by faith **plus** works! Yes, James teaches a works based salvation. Knowing the teaching of Paul concerning salvation from hell, which says we are saved by faith **alone** and *not of works* (cf. Eph 2:8-9), at first it seems the teaching of James presents a problem. Attempts to harmonize the apparent disparity between James and Paul are numerous. Some question the kind or quality of faith James discusses in verse 14, but that is not the issue. James in no way adds an adjective to classify some "form" of faith. Some say if one "truly" has faith [i.e. eternal life], then they will automatically produce works. But this is not what James is telling us. He is not telling us that faith naturally will or must provide works. If it does, then how much or many works should we expect? We know this because he has commanded us to not only be hearers but also doers. James commands Christians to perform works so they will be blessed. He is not going to command us to do something that simply comes naturally. Further, his command to produce works is not intended to make works a "verification system" for our eternal life. James **is not** saying we can have assurance of salvation from hell based upon our works. Such a system of verification would leave us hopelessly distraught. We would be wondering every day whether our works prove we were saved. Unfortunately, many do just this, never having assurance of eternal salvation from hell. Why? Because they are looking to themselves for proof – they have an incorrect understanding of the Scripture. The proof is in the promise of God through His Word! The work that saves us from hell is God's work. It was performed by God's Son upon the cross! This wonderful work is revealed to us through God's marvelous Word! James has already identified himself and his readers as those who have been born again by the will of the Father (1:18). Nothing is needed for assurance of salvation apart from believing the promise of God. God is faithful, and He can be trusted to perform above all others.

    Our common sense and logic lead us to recognize it is entirely possible to believe something yet not act upon it (we all believe things, but are not always obedient to act upon what we believe). But James emphatically is saying faith by itself cannot *save* us; it must have works. Again, James tells us faith by itself is unable to *save* us which is contrary to the teaching of Paul, or is it?

To help solve this mystery, it is important to examine the word *save*. To *save* means to rescue or deliver. The natural question is, *save* or deliver from what? Is James telling us that in order to be saved or delivered from hell, faith **and** works are required? Since he is addressing the *brethren* who have already been born again (cf. 1:18) and already saved from hell, he cannot be discussing salvation from hell. Salvation from hell has already occurred (cf. John 3:16-18, 36). This realization helps clear up a great deal of confusion. James must be talking about a different kind of salvation/deliverance. He is talking about deliverance from the death which can result when a Christian sins. He has already dealt with the death resulting from sin in a Christian's life in 1:13-16 (please refer back to Chapter 3 Evil, Sin, and Death). The ultimate deliverance a Christian needs is from himself and his sinful nature. As we obey God walking in His will, we will experience salvation day by day. As we persevere through this life, we can expect to experience salvation/deliverance at the Judgment Seat of Christ where we will receive reward for a job well done. This has been the context of James' epistle thus far, and it remains the burden of his writing.

To explain himself further, James gives the example in verses 15-16 of a person who is in need and is neglected by a Christian. We all need to be aware that love involves our action. When we possess the means and ability to help another person yet willingly choose not to do so, we are wrong. We all are more than likely guilty of this from time to time. When presented with an opportunity to minister, we may simply take the easy way out and declare "Oh my, I will pray for you." By not helping when we know we could and should help, we have not loved. Hence, James goes right back to the *Royal Law* of love. James says if you do not love your neighbor, you are committing sin. You are breaking the *Royal Law*. If you are not acting like the Good Samaritan, you are not loving and hence are not fulfilling the *Royal Law*. He ends v. 16 by again asking what profit or advantage is there in our lack of love (committing sin). The answer is obvious, none. Neither we nor anyone else we interact with benefit from our sin. A key to understanding James' point is his meaning of *profit*. To profit from something means to gain or obtain an advantage. Paul said, *and though I bestow all my goods to feed the poor, and though I give my body to be burned, and have not charity, it profiteth me nothing.* (1 Cor 13:3) Paul tells us even his own good works done without love are of no advantage to him. James and Paul both teach that works of love result in blessing or reward from the Lord (cf. 1:25).

Naturally, we can see faith without works does not achieve what God wants from us. James declares faith without works is dead or useless. God desires for us to act upon our faith so we will produce good works. Notice Paul's words regarding faith and works:

> [8]For by grace are ye saved through faith; and that not of yourselves: it is the gift of God: [9]Not of works, lest any man should boast. [10]For we are his workmanship, created in Christ Jesus unto good works, which God hath before ordained that we should walk in them. (Eph 2:8-10)

In context, Paul explains faith **without** works saves from hell. He then goes on to say the purpose for our salvation from hell is to act in a way pleasing to God. Paul tells us God has created us so that we should (not will, but should) produce good works. Good works are not automatic simply because of the faith that delivers us from hell. Faith alone saves from hell; good works **should** follow after this salvation. These good works produce the kind of fruit in our lives which our Lord desires. When we act upon our faith by producing good works, our Lord is glorified among men (cf. Matt 5:16). When James says faith without works is dead, he means the result is an unfruitful faith – faith that has not achieved its goal of producing works that give God the glory due His name. Another way to say it is, faith without works is useless or of no profit.

One way to visualize the correlation between faith and works or dead faith producing no works is to think of a bicycle.[1] Imagine saying we have a bicycle without a frame; do we really have a bicycle without a frame? No, we may have a few wheels, but we do not have a bicycle. On the other hand, if we visualize a bicycle but without a rider, we can equate it to faith without works. Once we envision a bicycle with a rider, we begin to see the potential for the bicycle to fulfill its purpose – for it to be alive and useful. Once the rider gets on the bicycle, he is able to take a trip and make use of the bicycle. So it is with faith and works, in order for our faith to be useful or profitable, we must act upon it in obedience. We must take it for a trip and ride it!

---

[1] Thanks to John Niemela for this example!

Sometimes we can get tripped up on the definition of a word. We can assign one definition to a word and not recognize the meaning of that word is mostly decided by its context. If we are not careful, we can read more into the words *save* and *dead* than James intends (or any other Biblical writer for that matter). For example, if I say "he is dead wrong" what do I mean? Obviously, I do not mean a physical kind of deadness. If I say "he is dead and they buried him yesterday," the context obviously shows physical death. When of Abraham and Sarah Paul said, *and being not weak in faith, he considered not his own body now **dead**, when he was about an hundred years old, neither yet the **deadness** of Sarah's womb* (Rom 4:19), he was not referring to physical or spiritual death. He was talking about a lack of ability. If I say, I was saved when I was ten years old, what do I mean? If that is all I said, you may ask "saved from what?" I could say, "I was saved by my brother from falling off the edge of a cliff," or I could say "I was saved from spending eternity in hell." Likewise, when Paul said *take heed unto thyself, and unto the doctrine; continue in them for in doing this thou shalt both save thyself, and them that hear thee* (1 Tim 4:16), what does he mean hear by *save*? The context suggests Paul is saying Timothy and his parishioners can be saved from the problems of false doctrine. From these examples we see words can have a wide range of meaning. So it is with James' use of *dead* and *save*.

To summarize, James is not saying the absence of works in our lives means we are without salvation from hell. If works are necessary to give or prove we have eternal life, then we are forever in despair. Every day we will be looking for good works to assure us of our eternal life. Graciously, God has freely given us eternal life! He then commands us to produce good works. If we do so, in His grace, God then promises to reward us for our good works. Not only has God been gracious to give us eternal life freely, He has also promised to present us with payment for faithful service to Him (cf. Heb 6:10; 10:35-36). James is careful to present the potential blessing of obedience to God we can enjoy. James admonishes Christians to practice their Christianity – to make it alive! The result provides benefits for everyone.

DISCUSSION QUESTIONS AND IDEAS

- Ask for examples of good works.
- Discuss what it means to profit or gain from doing good works.
- Give examples of ways we can show our faith rather than simply talk about it.
- Discuss the bicycle example and how it shows the purpose for our faith.
- Talk about the use of the word dead and how it has various meanings depending upon context.

CHAPTER 11
MATURE FAITH – IT WORKS

James 2:21-26

²¹Was not Abraham our father justified by works, when he had offered Isaac his son upon the altar? ²²Seest thou how faith wrought with his works, and by works was faith made perfect [mature]? ²³And the scripture was fulfilled which saith, Abraham believed God, and it was imputed unto him for righteousness: and he was called the Friend of God. ²⁴Ye see then how that by works a man is justified, and not by faith only. ²⁵Likewise also was not Rahab the harlot justified by works, when she had received the messengers, and had sent them out another way? ²⁶For as the body without the spirit is dead [unproductive or unfruitful], so faith without works is dead [unproductive or unfruitful] also.

We are about to complete the first section in the main body of the epistle of James. Remember the outline for the main body of the book is summarized in 1:19, *Wherefore, my beloved brethren, let every man be* **swift to hear, slow to speak, slow to wrath**. The first section on being *swift to hear* begins in 1:21 and ends with 2:26. James has been effectively teaching us how to be *swift to hear* in this section of his epistle. As we think back, James has told us not only to hear but to also do! In doing, he has revealed to us the importance of following the *Royal Law* of love. Thus, being swift to hear encompasses both listening and obeying

– hearing and doing. In our passage above, James vividly shows us mature faith by his example of Abraham and Rahab, two individuals in the Hebrews 11 faith "hall of fame." Consistent with our previous studies, James shows us the importance of maturing in the faith and the reward it brings. He also points out that if our faith is not accompanied by works, we are not progressing in our faith as we should. However, we must realize James does not tell us to attempt to determine the reality of our faith by examining our works. He knows his readers (and himself) have been born again because of their simple belief in Jesus Christ for the gift of eternal life (cf. 1:18). He is simply exhorting his readers to grow in their faith.

Before we examine this section of Scripture, we should look back at v. 18-20. In these verses James is using a literary style known as *diatribe* which introduces an objector – someone who objects to James' point about the relationship between faith and works. Notice the words of the objector in v. 18-19: *[18]...Thou hast faith, and I have works: shew me thy faith without thy works, and I will shew thee my faith by my works. [19]Thou believest that there is one God; thou doest well: the devils also believe, and tremble.* The entirety of verses 18-19 are the words of the objector. The words of the objector are evidenced by the introduction James provides in v. 18, *Yea, a man may say,* and end as James answers, *but wilt thou know, O vain man, that faith without works is dead* in v.20. In essence, the objector is saying there is no correlation between faith and works. This objector even tries to prove his point by referencing the belief of demons relative to their lack of good works. This is an absurd argument. James tells him there certainly is a correlation between faith and works; and this is where we pick up in verse 21.

James begins to refute the foolish man who objects to the faith/works connection. James tells him how works do justify a person. He goes on to say works bring faith to its goal – they make faith mature or perfect. He does this by using the most admired patriarch Abraham as an example. James uses the example of Abraham's offering of his son Isaac. However, Abraham had been justified by faith **alone** long before he was justified by works. Gen 15:6 tells us of Abraham's justification by faith **alone**. Paul uses this time in Abraham's life to describe for us how we are justified before God by faith alone – absent of works. Notice his words in the Book of Romans:

> ²For if Abraham were justified by works, he hath whereof to glory; but not before God. ³For what saith the scripture? Abraham believed God, and it was counted unto him for righteousness. ⁴Now to him that worketh is the reward not reckoned of grace, but of debt. ⁵But to him that worketh not, but believeth on him that justifieth the ungodly, his faith is counted for righteousness. (Rom 4:2-5)

Paul draws from Gen 15:6 to prove Abraham was justified by faith alone. This justification before God is relative to the gift of eternal life. Paul's teaching is that the one who simply believes the promise of God (cf. John 3:16; 6:47; Acts 16:31) has the gift of eternal life. Paul teaches we are justified by faith alone with this justification allowing us to stand before God **judicially** acceptable. This **judicial** acceptance is relative to the believer's position in Christ – our position as a child of God. It is absolutely, positively without works – nothing can be clearer than Paul's teaching in

Rom 4:2-5 and in various other passages (Rom 5:1; Eph 2:8-9; Titus 3:5).

What we should clearly see is the difference in time James uses as opposed to Paul. James does not deal with Abraham's faith in Gen 15:6. Rather, he catapults possibly 50 years later into Abraham's life when Abraham's name had been changed from Abram. Abraham had gone through various trials in His life and his faith had grown. He had walked with the Lord and produced good works. While originally Abraham believed God relative to the promise of a son (Gen 15:6; Rom 4:19-21), Abraham eventually believed in the resurrection of that very son (Gen 22:5; Heb 11:17-19). What a mighty growth in faith! Abraham was so convinced in the promises of God that he was willing to sacrifice the very son around whom the promises revolved! Abraham's faith was mature, and it had brought him to the place where God wanted him to be. Abraham's continued fellowship with the Lord had allowed him to come to the place of great faith! Greatness typifies Abraham, and he is rewarded with the title of *friend of God*.

We should also notice the justification James points out is a different justification than that of Paul in Romans 4. Paul's justification is through faith alone. James' justification is by faith and works. That two different justifications exist should be evident. James assumes justification by faith alone has already occurred in the life of his readers. He is dealing with their need for justification by works. One cannot be justified by works unless they have first been justified by faith alone. Justification by faith alone results in the gift of eternal life. Justification by works results in eternal reward.

Let's look closer at what James explains. He tells us Abraham was justified by works after he had offered Isaac on the altar in v. 21. He then proceeds to discuss a perfected faith in v. 22. The faith issue James is dealing with is one of perfected or matured faith. The word *perfect* in this passage denotes the idea of something being brought to an intended goal or the idea of something being fully developed. So, the faith Abraham had back in Gen 15:6, while not yet fully developed, had great potential. In Gen 22 it had matured and thus reached the purpose for which it was originally intended. Abraham's faith reached its intended goal and was fully developed. In v. 23 James explains that Abraham's initial faith revealed in Gen 15:6 reached its goal in his life. Abraham progressed in his walk with God earning the title of *friend of God* by his obedience. Hence, we can easily see what God began in Abraham had been brought to fruition. God had given Abraham the gift of eternal life along with various other promises. Abraham believed; and through numerous trials and errors, he developed a mature faith earning him one of the most favored titles in Scripture. God's work for Abraham had inspired Abraham to work for God. Because of Abraham's work, he was rewarded by God with commendation and a most enviable title.

The title of *friend of God* is something we as Christians should pursue. Jesus said, *Ye are my friends, if ye do whatsoever I command you.* (John 15:14) Just as Abraham earned the title *friend of God* by obedience, so can we. Just because we have the gift of eternal life does not mean God refers to us as His friend. Similarly, just because we have the gift of eternal life does not mean we love God. Our love for God and our friendship with God depends on our obedience to Him (cf. John 14:15). If we walk contrary to His will we are neither loving Him nor befriending Him. These titles and positions are conditioned on our obedience.

God wants us to love and befriend Him, but He does not force us to do so. Consequently, while we have the privilege of being God's friend, Scripture never insinuates God is our friend. Rather, God is the mighty Creator; He is the Lord of the entire universe. None are on His level. Thankfully, while He is so majestic, He is also benevolent – willing for any and all to befriend Him!

By this exposition from James, we see him continuing to emphasize the practical benefits of being a hearer and doer. He shows that blessing from God is the result of faithfulness on the part of the believer. God desires for our faith to be *alive* rather than *dead*. If we are obedient to His Word, our faith will be alive and fruitful. It will become mature reaching the intended goal of reward for perseverance – the *crown of life* (cf. 1:12). James shows us how our justification by works is very important as it will yield reward at the Judgment Seat of Christ. When we stand before our Lord at the Judgment Seat of Christ, our positional justification will most certainly be intact. The issue every Christian faces is whether our practical justification will be intact. Did we not only hear the Word, but did we do what it said – were we obedient? From our obedience we will be practically justified and worthy of reward (cf. John 12:25-26; 1 Pet 5:6).

One other example James gives concerning works based justification is the harlot Rahab. Rahab believed God and was also obedient. She was convinced the life of her and her family would be spared if she was faithful to help the spies. Heb 11:31 shows her initial faith when she *received the spies*. James describes this initial faith and also her matured faith when he says she had *sent them out another way.* Rahab not only believed God, she was faithful to do what she knew was right. Just like Abraham, Rahab developed a mature faith (albeit in a shorter time frame) and was rewarded by God with preservation of life as well as the commendation of a good name in Scripture. Hence, Rahab – no matter what her past contained – was a recipient of the grace of God. Her faith, followed by her actions (faithfulness), earned her practical justification.

    Finally, James gives us the analogy of how our body needs our spirit in order to operate. Without our spirit, our bodies are dead. As Christians, we need to remain *alive* in faith. In this first section on being *swift to hear*, James has given us precious instruction on how to have a vibrant faith. The good works he describes are simple and straight forward. We are to practice *pure religion* by caring for those less fortunate while remaining pure from worldly influences (1:27). Partiality towards others should have no place in our lives (2:1). Of course our main operative is love! When we act out of love, we have certainly done good works (2:8). All of our works should be done in light of the instruction of Scripture. Obedience to the revealed will of God is most certainly good works.

    We do not need to break fellowship with the Lord for the result is death – a dead faith. If we are hearers and not doers then our faith will begin atrophying or wasting away. This is not the intended purpose for our lives. God desires for us to be alive and fruitful. He desires for our walk to be onward and upward as we mature in faith. Truly, a mature faith works!

DISCUSSION QUESTIONS AND IDEAS

- Ask for examples of good works.
- Give examples of good works a person can perform.
- Discuss what it means to earn the title *friend of God*.
- Discuss the importance of having a faith that is alive and active as opposed to dead and inactive.
- Provide advice on how believers can mature in their faith.

CHAPTER 12
THE PERFECT MAN

James 3:1-2

¹My brethren, be not many masters, knowing that we shall receive the greater condemnation [judgment]. ²For in many things we offend all. If any man offend not in word, the same is a perfect [mature] man, and able also to bridle the whole body.

Beginning in Chapter 3, James moves on to a new section in his epistle. His emphasis is now upon what we say – the control of our mouth! James knew the power of words and how they have lasting effect. The whole of Chapter 3 – all eighteen verses – deal with the subject of controlling our mouth. Remember, James does not haphazardly move into this area. His sermon is well thought out. His outline for the book is found in 1:19 where it says, *Wherefore, my beloved brethren, let every man be swift to hear,* **slow to speak***, slow to wrath.* Being *slow to speak* is the topic James covers more fully in Chapter 3.

Before we move forward in Chapter 3, let's review James' first section (1:21-2:26). James has skillfully addressed the concept of being *swift to hear*. As we have seen, James' idea of being *swift to hear* includes listening and doing. The doing includes helping the poor and needy. It involves fair and righteous treatment of all people. It means we observe the most important part of the *Royal Law* – love. We are to act just as Christ did and instructed. He commanded us to love one another, to have compassion, to forgive, and to serve. James has given us numerous practical situations to consider as we evaluate our own actions. We must also remember James has addressed believers – those who are born again. Numerous times he encourages us to be faithful and obedient. James concluded his section on being *swift to hear* by telling us to have faith which is alive and working. He did not tell us if our faith is not working and hence dead, then we were lost people. Quite the contrary, James tells us (believers) we need to be doers and not hearers only. Our works need to compliment what we believe (our faith) and bring our faith to its intended goal – good works that please God and are rewarded by Him.

Please do not take James' words about dead faith and conclude that if your works do not measure up, then you have not been born again. Rather, allow James' words to do what they were intended to do – to change your mind and actions so that you are a loving, compassionate, and forgiving Christian who is displaying your faith to all around. Be *alive* in the Lord! Allow your faith to be fruitful, producing good works so others can glorify your Father in heaven.

The control of our tongue is an age-old issue. Many times we do not necessarily live our lives as we should, but we talk about how others should live their lives. In the absence of our works there is many times an abundance of words. Hence, in many ways our works and words do not compliment our faith. An uncontrolled tongue can be devastating. Its power, as James will tell us, is great. We all have had various experiences in our lives where what someone said to us changed our lives – for the good or bad. As Christians, we need to guard our tongue making sure we speak the truth in love (cf. Eph 4:15). Jesus told us we will be judged based on what we say (cf. Matt 12:36). With this in mind, we should seek the wisdom and guidance of God's Word through His messenger James.

James begins his discussion of the tongue in a unique manner. He first points out the responsibility of teachers. James includes himself as he discusses the severity and responsibility of teaching. A paraphrase of 3:1 is, "Brothers and sisters in Christ, think carefully before you become a Bible teacher, because you know what you say will be judged more strictly by the Lord." The word *masters* in the KJV is the word for teachers used elsewhere in the NT. It is used interchangeably with the word for *rabbi*. Also, the word *condemnation* in the KJV is the word for judgment.

Those who are teachers, or lead other people, have great influence. Leadership via teaching is not something anyone should enter into lightly. Rather, it should be entered into with humility and Godly fear. With the privilege comes responsibility. Not only must a teacher edify in love, they also must teach the truth. If either of these is missing, James tells us to expect strict judgment.

As we consider James' words here, we should reflect on the time and culture of his original readers. They were on the heels of the risen Lord (possibly only a few years after His resurrection) and greatly influenced by Jewish tradition. Being NT believers, they were some of the original individuals who now comprised the newly formed *body of Christ*. While they were Jews by physical birth, they were now members of the body of Christ via the second birth (1:18). Knowing this, we should realize the assembly of these believers was very different than our assemblies today. They were much less structured, having no church buildings where everyone gathered. Most likely, they met in homes or even outside. Also, remember James writes to those *scattered abroad* (1:1). These believers are away from their homeland and possibly from their friends and family. When they met to worship together, many times men would rise and admonish the group. The problem James may have been addressing was the number of "volunteer" teachers who rose to instruct the other believers. James warns them of the accountability teachers have when they stand before the Lord at the Judgment Seat of Christ.

In his epistles, Paul revealed not every believer has the spiritual gift of teaching. While every believer has a spiritual gift or gifts, not every believer has been given the gift of teaching. All believers have God ordained gift(s). These gifts are given for the edification or improvement of the *body of Christ*. Believers do not choose their gifts, rather they are given sovereignly by the Lord as He sees fit (cf. 1 Cor 12:11, 18).

If one is bestowed with the gift of teaching, they must realize both the privilege and responsibility they have. James indicates the judgment bar is set higher for them. This is nothing new, for Jesus had already pointed out the consequences of incorrect teaching (cf. Matt 5:19). In 1 Corinthians 3, Paul discusses our service to the Lord in light of our Lord's evaluation of our works at the Judgment Seat of Christ. In 1 Cor 3:9-15 Paul is specifically speaking to pastors and teachers. While there is certainly application to every believer, he specifically addresses pastors and teachers regarding their ministry efforts. This is sobering and should cause teachers to evaluate themselves daily in light of the most important day of their lives – the Day of Christ (cf. Phil 1:6, 10; 2:16; 2 Thes 2:2) otherwise known as the Judgment Seat of Christ. As we remember, James has been focused on this Day of Judgment since the beginning of his epistle. James' mind was upon pleasing the Lord and subsequently receiving the *crown of life* (1:12) for a job well done. Without question, this one theme should dominate all we say and do as Christians (cf. 1 Cor 9:24-27; Phil 3:11-14; Col 3:23-25).

As a teacher, one should live his life in submission to the Lord. Like Paul, teachers should strive to discipline themselves (cf. 1 Cor 9:27) so they are rewarded by the Lord for a job well done. If teachers are doing this, they will not only be able to speak the truth in love, but they will also be a living example of how others are to live the Christian life. If teachers are obedient to the Lord, they can say to students "be like me because I am emulating Christ" or "follow me because I am following Christ." Notice what Paul said concerning this in 1 Cor 4:16, *be ye followers of me*. Paul was a living example of faithfulness, and he was not ashamed to share his example with others. Observe his words to the Ephesian Church:

> [17]And from Miletus he sent to Ephesus, and called the elders of the church. [18]And when they were come to him, he said unto them, Ye know, from the first day that I came into Asia, after what manner I have been with you at all seasons, [19]Serving the LORD with all humility of mind, and with many tears, and temptations, which befell me by the lying in wait of the Jews: [20]And how I kept back nothing that was profitable unto you, but have

shewed you, and have taught you publicly, and from house to house. (Acts 20:17-20)

Also notice what he said in 2 Thes 2:10, *Ye are witnesses, and God also, how holily and justly and unblameably we behaved ourselves among you that believe.* Paul knew of his responsibility and accountability to God. He knew the importance of serving the Lord with fear (cf. 2 Cor 5:8-11). He wanted all his followers to stand before the Lord with confidence (cf. Phil 1:10; 1 Thes 5:23; 1 John 2:28). By his example and teaching, Paul knew those whom he influenced could be awarded a *crown* (1:12) and commendation (Matt 25:21) from the Lord. He also knew he could influence others to stumble, thus causing harm for them and himself on that great Day of Judgment.

This short sentence (3:1) reveals much for us. We should daily seek the Lord with humility and fear. If we are teachers, we should be especially careful to discipline ourselves in the Lord. If we are not teachers, then we should especially hold up in prayer the teachers in our lives. Humility, compassion, love, forgiveness, and faithfulness should characterize our lives. What we say should be backed up by what we do. Teacher or not, we should never say 'do as I say, not as I do.' Our personal behavior is a great teacher in and of itself.

The position of teacher is not one of prestige. Rather it is one of piety. While the responsibility is great, so is the potential for blessing. Our Lord gives us blessing in this life that helps us continue on. But the primary blessing that should motivate us is the commendation "well done" which we can most surely look forward to when we stand before our righteous loving Judge.

Before all teachers become paralyzed with fear, they should read 3:2. He tells us we all make mistakes. Be sure, for James includes himself in the admonition. If we are human, we are going to make mistakes. We are all going to say and do things we wish we could take back. When we make mistakes, we are to acknowledge them and deal with them appropriately. The important thing is to be aware carefully to keeping mistakes to a minimum.

James' emphasis continues to be on the tongue. In verse two he tells us we can control our entire body with our tongue. He will expand upon this concept in the following verses. But as a way of introduction, James says the one who controls his tongue is *perfect*. This word *perfect* is the Greek word *teleios* which means flawless, but not sinless. It carries the idea of maturity and being blameless. As we shall see, James continues to deal with practical issues related to our Christian walk. We must not forget his context concerning faith which is alive and useful as opposed to dead and unfruitful.

The way we use the word *perfect* in English many times skews our understanding of the Biblical teaching on perfection. In Biblical usage, the word *perfect* very seldom refers to sinless perfection. Rather, it usually refers to maturity and completion. It carries the idea of being fully grown. Jesus told us, *Be ye therefore **perfect**, even as your Father which is in heaven is **perfect***. (Matt 5:48). Jesus did not mean we were to be sinless like our Father. He meant we were to be mature in the context of love and forgiveness as is our Heavenly Father. This perfection is not something achieved overnight – it is a process.

Paul made numerous references to perfection among the brethren. He connected this perfection to our daily lives – not to our judicial position in Christ. His teaching comes directly from and in concert with Jesus. The perfection to which Paul refers is Christian maturity. Notice what he says:

> Howbeit we speak wisdom among them that are **perfect** (1 Cor 2:6); Till we all come in the unity of the faith, and of the knowledge of the Son of God, unto a **perfect** man, unto the measure of the stature of the fullness of Christ. (Eph 4:13); [27]To whom God would make known what is the riches of the glory of this mystery among the Gentiles; which is Christ in you, the hope of glory: [28]Whom we preach, warning every man, and teaching every man in all wisdom; that we may present every man **perfect** in Christ Jesus: (Col 1:27-28); [16]All scripture is given by inspiration of God, and is profitable for doctrine, for reproof, for correction, for instruction in righteousness: [17]That the man of God may be **perfect**, thoroughly furnished unto all good works. [Emphasis mine] (2 Tim 3:16-17)

The teaching of perfection or maturity is abundant in the Bible. It is the goal for which we are all to strive. If we are maturing in the faith, then our faith is alive and working as it should. If we begin to backslide, our faith dies, and our works become sinful and unprofitable. No doubt about it, our goal should be to mature in Christ.

James tells us if we are mature, we will be able to control our tongue. If we do so, we will be able to also control the rest of our body (our total person). How can this be? What does James mean? First, James is not saying we should become paranoid over the issue of perfection. We are going to sin. James already knew the truth John later revealed: *If we confess our sins, he is faithful and just to forgive us our sins, and to cleanse us from all unrighteousness.* (1 John 1:9) In light of this glorious truth we are to seek maturity and wisdom. We do this by communing with our Lord via prayer and Bible study. There really is no other way to be mature. God's Word will change us as we study and become obedient to its instruction. In light of this, James shows how our tongue reveals our heart. What comes out of our mouth proceeds from our heart. Jesus told us, *out of the abundance of the heart the mouth speaketh.* (Matt 12:34b)[1] When and how we speak reveals the closeness of our walk with the Lord. So, to the extent we bridle our tongue, we display our maturity in the Lord. This control results from close communion with our Lord.

Because of these truths, we should strive for perfection/maturity. Striving for this is wise. It means accepting our faults and not being discouraged because of them. It means we should live with the intention of overcoming our faults as we grow in the Lord. It means we know the Lord loves us in spite of our faults and has made a way for us to excel towards maturity.

---

[1] The heart, eyes, and other tangible body parts are many times used to describe our mind in Scripture (cf. Eph 1:18; Rom 10:10; 12:2). Our mind operates in a non tangible way and is a function of our soul. Our heart, as an organ, does not think nor have cognition. Neither does the fat that makes up our brain. So, when the Scripture says believe with your heart, it metaphorically refers to our mind, since neither the heart muscle nor our brain fat have any ability in and of themselves to communicate to others or relate to God. The interaction of our body, soul, and spirit are mysterious and sometimes difficult to understand or delineate (cf. Heb 4:12).

DISCUSSION QUESTIONS AND IDEAS

- Ask for examples of how a teacher/coach/parent has had a positive effect on someone.
- Discuss the importance of controlling our tongue.
- Give an example of how someone has said something to you that encouraged you or even changed your life for the better.
- Give some examples of mature behavior and how it is beneficial as opposed to immature behavior.
- Talk about practical ways to avoid the misuse of our tongue: planned daily communion with the Lord (this includes confession of sins of our tongue and a request for help); planned Bible reading and study; regular participation in Bible study classes; changing who you hang around with...getting new friends with the proper influence.

CHAPTER 13
THE BIG MOUTH

James 3:3-12

³Behold, we put bits in the horses' mouths, that they may obey us; and we turn about their whole body. ⁴Behold also the ships, which though they be so great, and are driven of fierce winds, yet are they turned about with a very small helm, whithersoever the governor listeth. ⁵Even so the tongue is a little member, and boasteth great things. Behold, how great a matter a little fire kindleth! ⁶And the tongue is a fire, a world of iniquity: so is the tongue among our members, that it defileth the whole body, and setteth on fire the course of nature; and it is set on fire of hell. ⁷For every kind of beasts, and of birds, and of serpents, and of things in the sea, is tamed, and hath been tamed of mankind: ⁸But the tongue can no man tame; it is an unruly evil, full of deadly poison. ⁹Therewith bless we God, even the Father; and therewith curse we men, which are made after the similitude of God. ¹⁰Out of the same mouth proceedeth blessing and cursing. My brethren, these things ought not so to be. ¹¹Doth a fountain send forth at the same place sweet water and bitter? ¹²Can the fig tree, my brethren, bear olive berries? either a vine, figs? so can no fountain both yield salt water and fresh.

As we ponder verses 3-12, we cannot help but identify with the power of the tongue! James really has a great way of showing us our "big mouth." These verses are right in the middle of James' section on being *slow to speak* (1:19). In verses 3-12, James expands upon the power of our tongue as it relates to our daily lives. He tells us how our tongue sets the course for our lives in many ways. He generally speaks in a negative light concerning the tongue. What we say tends to corrupt our whole person. James metaphorically says the tongue is on fire from hell. He then correlates what we sometimes say to deadly poison. Then, he shows how our tongue can be hypocritical. We can bless and curse in the same breath. James tells us this should not be so. Speaking to the *brethren*, James says watch your "big mouth!"

Control, we all want to be in control. Certainly, God is in control, and we have been made in His likeness. But, even though we are made in His likeness, sin has defaced us. While His likeness has not been obliterated in us, we have been spoiled by sin. In verses 3-4, James describes a few things in the world to convey the idea of control – the bit in a horse's mouth and the rudder on a ship. Both are very small compared to what they control. But both in fact have great control over direction. James' point is rather simple and helps us understand the importance of the "little things" in our lives. Our tongue – really what we say with our tongue – has great power. James shows us the great potential of the tongue in the first part of v. 5.

In the second part of verse 5, James makes a transition. Referring to the tongue, he says it *boasteth great things*. Now he begins to explain the potential danger associated with an unruly tongue. Remember, James is speaking to the *brethren*. We must not be fooled into thinking if our tongue is out of control, we are not *brethren*. Quite the contrary, saved people struggle to control their tongue every day. So do not doubt your salvation because you may say or think sinful things. Your salvation is based solely on the finished work of Christ. We have discussed this truth in prior chapters, but it is important we always remember the security we have because of God's work for us!

When our "big mouth" is open, we have trouble. Not only do we have trouble, but those around us have trouble. We must realize what we say affects others – sometimes greatly. Our mouth can be used for good or bad. It can *speak the truth in love* (Eph 4:15) or it can spread judgment and discouragement like a *deadly poison*. When we fail to speak the truth in love, we grieve the Spirit. He is sensitive and does not enjoy when our mouths spew forth poisonous words infecting those around us. Paul tells us to keep our mouth clean and use it for good. He says for us to *grieve not the spirit of God* (Eph 4:29-30). If we grieve the Spirit, we are automatically out of fellowship with the Lord. In order to restore fellowship, we must confess our sin (cf. 1 John 1:9). Hence, we need to realize the danger our "big mouth" represents!

What we say – to a great extent – controls how we act. An example of self-talk is revealing. If every morning we arise and say to ourselves, 'I am a no good sinner and my life is not worth living,' how do you think our day will go? Will we be in a mind set to love and encourage other sinners? Of course not. However, if every morning we arise and say, 'While still a sinner, I have been saved by God from the lake of fire and can be used by God even though I have faults,' how do you think our day will go? What will our actions tend to be like? If we say, 'I can so please God today by obeying His commandments, that He will love me extra special and reward me for my actions,' how will that affect our actions? Take that a step further, how will our outlook affect others...how will what we say and think influence others? The power of simply what we say affects everyone. Further, what is most important is this, we must speak the truth! We should *speak the truth in love* to ourselves and to others. The Scriptures are truth, and from them we can make truthful statements!

In verse 6, James explains the potential danger of our tongue. He likens our tongue to fire. It does not take much fire to start a major forest fire which can destroy thousands of acres. So is our tongue when it is out of control. It is a *world of iniquity* as James says. He reveals how our tongue is capable of igniting any sin you can imagine! Yes, this is even true of Christians. The tongue is dangerous and can be greatly influenced by Satan. When Peter began to correct the Lord Jesus concerning His declaration of suffering and death on the cross, Jesus told Peter, *get thee behind me Satan* (Matt 16:23). Just prior to this influence of Satan, Peter had been greatly influenced by the Father when he declared the great truth concerning Jesus' identity, *thou art the Christ, the Son of the Living God* (Matt 16:16). How quickly the influence changed and his mind and mouth were subject to truth and falsehood.

In verses 7-8 James continues to discuss the deadly potential of the tongue. He declares the tongue is unable to be controlled. The animals of nature can be controlled but man's tongue is uncontrollable. It is unruly and likened to a deadly poison. James' figurative language is dreadfully descriptive. He is passionate about helping us see how dangerous our "big mouth" can be! Prov 18:21 declares, d*eath and life are in the power of the tongue.* By being so vivid and passionate, James attempts to show us the severity of our sinfulness. Remember, he is speaking to born again children of God. James wants us to become convicted of our sinful "big mouth" and do something about it.

Until we see ourselves for who we are – sinful and in need of constant fellowship with God – we will continue to have a problem with our tongue. A somber but very effective message; one which caused Paul to say he was the chief of sinners (1 Tim 1:15)! When we recognize our sinful nature on a daily basis, it will propel us to avail ourselves of the ministry of our Great High Priest (cf. Heb 4:14-16). He will help us in our time of need!

This sorrow for sin is a key to controlling our tongue and hence, our actions. The Prophet Daniel knew this and was a man of sorrow and confession. Although there are not any of Daniel's sins ever revealed in Scripture, he certainly confessed his sin and the sin of Israel (cf. Dan 9:3-20). Because of his broken and contrite spirit, Daniel was exceedingly endowed with knowledge and wisdom from the Lord. The same heart of contrition can be seen in Isaiah. He declared, *woe is me! For I am undone; because I am a man of unclean lips.* (Isa 6:5) Both Isaiah and Daniel were men of greatness because they both knew of their great sinfulness. The good news is that God is a grand forgiver of sin. Paul proclaimed, *where sin abounded, grace did much more abound.* (Rom 5:20)

Notice how James includes himself by saying *we*. We can bless the Lord, and then curse others. James reveals the sin of cursing others. He affirms the truth that human beings are made in the image of God. When we gossip against or defame others, we are actually cursing God's creation. Every person is important to God. God loves us so much that He *commendeth his love toward us, in that, while we were yet sinners, Christ died for us.* (Rom 5:8) God sent His Son, the Lord Jesus Christ, so each and every human being could be saved from eternal damnation (cf.

John 3:16; 1 Tim 2:4). Hence, every human being is important to God.

To curse others, at its most basic level is to find fault with them. It is to point out they are not perfect. Why do we so often want to find fault? It is generally because of our own insecurity. When we begin to speak negatively of others, we are trying to exalt ourselves. We are trying to cover up our own imperfections. When we put others down, we reveal how low we actually are ourselves. Instead of put downs, our words to others should be pickups. The saying from Thumper's father, "if you can't say something nice, then don't say anything at all," contains great wisdom. If we refrain from speaking evil, we can refrain from doing evil.

James explains blessing and cursing from a Christian should not occur! Verses 9-12 show how contradictory blessing and cursing are. James does not say it is impossible for Christians to have this struggle. In fact, he is attempting to correct this problem among the brethren. Again, we must realize that the moment we were born again, we did not attain sinless perfection nor were we fully grown in the faith. Unfortunately, many have this kind of theology, even though they will not come out and say it. Many think that since God has saved us He will do everything for us. We must not be deceived into thinking this falsehood. Satan has done a masterful job of corrupting the simplicity that is in Christ. As Christians, we are commanded to do many things. We cannot simply follow the old adage "let go and let God." This concept in many ways is a cop out. God is at work in us, but He commands us to be at work in concert with Him. Until we see our responsibility as Christians, then our lives will be a wreck. We must do many things; James has instructed us to be not only *hearers* but also *doers*. In doing so, God will bless us (cf. 1:22-25)! So realize we cannot simply say 'Lord, you live my life for me.' No, God is telling us He will energize us to live our Christian life, if we abide in Him and keep His commandments.[1]

In an effort to control our "big mouth," we sometimes try to get involved with church work. Maybe we have the gift of teaching, and think if we start teaching our life will be better. Of course, the gifts and calling of God are without repentance (Rom 11:29). In other words, God does not remove our spiritual abilities just because we sin. We can use our gifts for God's glory and still be sinful with little to no change in our lives. Paul revealed this truth as he explained the importance of practicing what he preached (cf. 1 Cor 9:27). Paul knew he had to discipline himself. His part of the work was to obey God's commandments. Paul knew even though he was extremely gifted, it would not win him the *crown* he so desperately wanted to win (cf. 1 Cor 9:24-27; Phil 3:11-14; 2 Tim 4:6-8). His performance energized by God would decide his reward.

Moral piety is commanded by Scripture. We are commanded to live holy lives. We are to be conformed to the image of Christ rather than to the image of the world system. Many times we think we are pleasing God because we do not drink, smoke, live licentiously, or commit outwardly open sins. While living holy in this manner is important, it does not mean we are truly pious or as James puts it, have *pure religion* (1:27). James has told us that even though we do not commit the big sins (adultery, murder, etc.) we still break the law if we fail to love one

---

[1] Refer back to Chapter 6 *Hearing and Doing* for a discussion of the Synergistic Christian Life.

another (cf. 2:8-13). Our love for God is evidenced by our love for fellow believers. The apostle John makes this point in 1 John 4:19-21. The main way we show love for fellow believers is how we talk to them. While we can live outward lives of piety, if we are not showing love via our tongue, we are deceiving ourselves. Christians need to take to heart the "little things" and realize God's primary commandment for us is love! If we are loving others, we are loving God and thus in fellowship with Him. The converse is also true. Actually, the "little things" aren't so little!

Controlling our mouth is up to us. We must rely on the Lord for help, but we cannot expect Him to just do it as we sit passively by. If we think we do not have to contribute, then we will experience a life of failure. Our appearance before the Judgment Seat of Christ will be one of shame (cf. 1 John 2:28). So, how do we control this incontrollable "big mouth?" First, we must realize we have responsibility in the matter. Second, we must realize and confess our utter sinfulness. Third, we must seek the Lord in daily prayer and study. Jesus said, *watch and pray that you enter not into temptation.* (Matt 26:41) As we do these things we will be cognizant of our dangerous tongue. Moses, the great servant of the Lord, *spake unadvisedly with his lips.* (Ps 106:33) We will go to our grave with the battle, but we can win! The Lord has promised we will not be tempted with something we cannot overcome (cf. 1 Cor 10:13). Our job is to remain positive and believe God. When we believe Him, we can then be obedient. Along with this outlook, we must also be fearful of the dangers of allowing our "big mouth" to rule us. The Lord is going to judge us for *every idle word.* (Matt 12:36) We should allow fear to have its proper place. Godly fear produces holiness and truth in our lives (cf. Heb 12:28-29). We must also remember we are in a war (cf. Eph 6:12). It is a cosmic war, and our enemy is exceedingly powerful. Our enemy is staunchly against us because God is for us. Satan wants to rob us of all that God wants for us. Satan wants to take our *crown* (cf. Rev 3:11) while God wants to award us a *crown* and commendation (1:12; 2 Tim 4:6-8; Matt 25:21).

Do not be discouraged by the fact you have a "big mouth!" Be encouraged that you know the truth about it! Know God is for you and wants you to be victorious. In His wisdom He has allowed us to battle with our "big mouth." He wants us to avail ourselves of His resources so we can be victorious and earn the *crown of life* (cf. 1:12). To do so requires our participation and perseverance. We must know the danger and use the tools God has in grace given.

DISCUSSION QUESTIONS AND IDEAS

- Give examples of how even a small child can "control" things with their mouth.
- Ask for or give examples of the power of simply saying something and how it motivates for the good or bad.
- Discuss sinfulness and how it is in all of us.
- Ask for examples of big sins and little sins; point out how we can think we are righteous but ignore sins of our tongue.
- Give an example of how you refrained from saying something (hopefully this has happened at least once!), and it made a big difference.
- Give the plan for being victorious over the "big mouth".

CHAPTER 14
WISE MEN

James 3:13-18

¹³Who is a wise man and endued with knowledge [understanding] among you? let him shew out of a good conversation [conduct] his works with meekness of wisdom. ¹⁴But if ye have bitter envying and strife in your hearts, glory not, and lie not against the truth. ¹⁵This wisdom descendeth not from above, but is earthly, sensual, devilish [demonic]. ¹⁶For where envying and strife is, there is confusion and every evil work. ¹⁷But the wisdom that is from above is first pure, then peaceable, gentle, and easy to be intreated [willing to yield], full of mercy and good fruits, without partiality, and without hypocrisy. ¹⁸And the fruit of righteousness is sown in peace of them that make peace.

Having thoroughly discussed the power of the "big mouth" in 3:3-12, James asks a question, *who is wise among you?* After describing what a foolish Christian does – use their tongue for their own interests and lusts – James wants to know if there are any among the congregation who are wise. The wise one will not be self serving. The wise one is able to delay gratification. The wise ones do not have to always have it their way. The wise one does not fall prey to the "big mouth" syndrome. This should be our aspiration as Christians – to be called wise! Let's explore

James' sermon more and focus on where we need to change so we can one day hear the commendation "well done, thou wise and faithful servant" (Luke 12:42-44).

Just how important is it for a Christian to be wise? When we were born again (cf. 1:18; John 3:3), we became children of God who then needed to grow up in the Lord. Christian maturity is the path every Christian should be running upon. Unfortunately, many do not see the value of having wisdom. Many think they do not have what it takes to be called wise. This is sad because God has commanded us to be wise. He has commanded us to grow up in Him! Further, He has graciously given us everything necessary to become wise.

Wisdom is defined as **experiential or properly applied knowledge** (cf. Prov 1:1-6). It results in "skilled living." Wisdom involves **intelligence and moral integrity** (cf. Prov 8:7-9). Wisdom involves **expertise and discipline** in all areas of life! Wisdom yields a life of **discipline and order** pleasing to God. Wisdom begins with a **fear of the Lord** (cf. Prov 9:10). Godly fear is reverential awe and respect. Fear is a God given motivator for holy living (cf. Heb 12:28-29).

God has not commanded us to do something we are unable to do. While we all have different circumstances, the Lord's desire is for us to bloom where we are planted. Our potential for growth can be likened to much of God's creation. Take for example a beautiful flower. A majestic rose does not simply appear one day. For a rose to achieve its beauty and splendor, it must first begin as a seed in the ground. Covered by dirt rich in nutrients along with a consistent amount of moisture, the seed has time to develop. Without the proper amount of nutrients and water, the seed will not develop to its full potential.

It will be stunted in growth if the right ingredients are withheld. However, if the proper nutrients are present, over time a beautiful majestic rose, which is pleasing to the eyes and nose, will develop. God is good, and His creation is wondrous!

Just as God provides for the rose, so does He for His children (cf. Matt 6:25-34). God has given four primary ingredients that allow for the growth and maturity of His children:

1. His holy Word (John 17:17)
2. His Holy Spirit (John 16:8-14)
3. His holy angels (Heb 1:14)
4. His holy people (Heb 10:24-25)

Yes, God has given these things, and each person is able to mature. Differing amounts of ingredients are necessary for most of us. Not everyone has the same circumstances, knowledge, intellect, abilities, etc. However, God knows exactly what we need. He is able to take us where we need to go. He does not place upon us things which will cause us not to grow. In fact, He places obstacles in our way so we will grow. If we remember back to Chapter 1, James told us to rejoice in trials because of the benefit trials bring (1:1-12). Trials bring patience, and patience works maturity in us. The end result for the Christian who is patient, loving, and mature is the *crown of life*. God rewards His children for their perseverance in the faith. By graciously providing the four primary ingredients listed above, He has "pulled out all the stops" for us so that we may become wise.

An entire genre of literature in the Old Testament is known as the wisdom literature (Job, Psalms, Proverbs, Ecclesiastes, and Song of Solomon). In that selection, the Book of

Proverbs stands out with a special emphasis on wisdom for believers. It is important we as believers realize our need to seek wisdom. We must not think we are wise simply because we know the Lord as our Savior. Being born again does not necessarily equate to being wise. Rather, wisdom is something for which we are to attain. It takes our work and dedication. We must seek to be wise – we must search diligently for wisdom.

Notice a few of the verses which describe wisdom from the book of Proverbs:

> The fear of the Lord is the beginning of knowledge; but fools despise wisdom and instruction. (1:7); Happy is the man that findeth wisdom: and the man that getteth understanding. (3:13); The wise shall inherit glory: but shame shall be the promotion of fools. (3:35); Wisdom is the principal thing; therefore get wisdom: and with all thy getting get understanding. Exalt her, and she shall promote thee: she shall bring thee to honor, when thou dost embrace her. She shall give to thine head an ornament of grace: a crown of glory shall she deliver to thee. (4:7-9)

If wisdom is the principal thing, should not we all be focused upon wisdom? Of course we should! But why does it evade many? Why are some Christians living defeated lives – foolish lives? There are several reasons, but I believe the main reason is a lack of faith! Most Christians believe God has the power to give them eternal life (however, if they have never believed this, then they are not born again)! Beyond the power to give eternal life, many do not believe they can grow much further. Many look to their utter sinfulness and say, "what is the use?" Maybe they say so because they have fallen back into sinful habits, not seeing a way out. Well, good news is revealed in God's Word. If we believe God for wisdom, He will give it (1:5-6). Of course, wisdom does not simply drop out of the sky by way of carrier pigeon! Nor does it come in a high priority email or immediate heavenly 4G download! Wisdom comes through trials. Wisdom comes through obedience to the Lord. Obtaining wisdom takes diligence on our part.

Wisdom must be sought after. Notice the words of Solomon:

> ^{1}My son, if thou wilt receive my words, and hide my commandments with thee; ^{2}So that thou incline thine ear unto wisdom, and apply thine heart to understanding; ^{3}Yea, if thou criest after knowledge, and liftest up thy voice for understanding; ^{4}If thou seekest her as silver, and searchest for her as for hid treasures; ^{5}Then shalt thou understand the fear of the LORD, and find the knowledge of God. ^{6}For the LORD giveth wisdom: out of his mouth cometh knowledge and understanding. ^{7}He layeth up sound wisdom for the righteous: he is a buckler to them that walk uprightly. ^{8}He keepeth the paths of judgment, and preserveth the way of his saints. ^{9}Then shalt thou understand righteousness, and judgment, and equity; yea, every good path. ^{10}When wisdom entereth into thine heart, and knowledge is

pleasant unto thy soul; ¹¹Discretion shall preserve thee, understanding shall keep thee. (Prov 2:1-11)

Wow! What great advice from Solomon to his son. Certainly, by application we can understand these words as being to us from our Heavenly Father. He cares for us and wants us to be wise. We can see the parallel thoughts from this section of Proverbs with the book of James. In Prov 2:1 we are told to receive the Word of God. This is the same thing James told us when he said, *receive with meekness the engrafted [implanted] word, which is able to save your souls.* (1:21). Receiving the Word of God is the first step to wisdom. But in order to receive the Word, we must actually read it. Receiving the Word means to allow it to settle in and change our lives. In fact, James says it will save our lives [souls]. The deliverance our souls can expect is from our present life of sin and degradation to a life of fullness and reward. The *crown of life* will be ours if we finish our course with wisdom.

Beyond simply reading the Word, we must study, ponder, and meditate upon it. Becoming wise takes a great deal of work on our part. Prov 2:2 tells us to incline our ears to wisdom and to be diligent in our hearts [our minds] to understand that which the Lord has for us. Prov 2:3-4 says to lay aside everything else and make the pursuit of wisdom our priority. If we want wisdom, we must go looking for it. We must desire it as a prized possession worthy of our most diligent efforts. If that is the case, we will obtain wisdom. We will understand what it means to fear the Lord. Fearing the Lord means just what it says. If we fear the Lord, we are scared of Him! We are scared of not pleasing Him. When we fear Him it changes our sinful lives. Fear of the Lord leads us to shun sin and follow righteousness. Fearing the Lord propels us to deeper depths and higher heights in our Christian life. Solomon sums up the topic when he says,

> [13] Let us hear the conclusion of the whole matter: Fear God, and keep his commandments: for this is the whole duty of man. [14] For God shall bring every work into judgment, with every secret thing, whether it be good, or whether it be evil. (Eccl 12:13-14)

Knowing we are God's children, we should fear the Lord, because we know He is also our Judge! We should live our lives in light of His all seeing eye, knowing He rewards righteous acts but punishes sinful acts (cf. Rom 14:8-12; Col 3:23-25; 2 Cor 5:8-11). When we know and accept this truth, it will change our lives. We will truly find the knowledge of God! We will be wise!

The wise person will show his wisdom – the beginning of which is a healthy fear of the Lord – by his actions (cf. 3:13b). The wise one will be meek and willing to serve others. Meekness is not weakness. In fact, meekness is a display of power under control. The wise one is filled with the Holy Spirit (because he has spent time in the Word and in prayer) being led by the Spirit. The lust of the flesh does not control him, rather the fruit of the Spirit is emanating from him (cf. Gal 5:13-26; Rom 8:1-17).

In verses 14-16, James shows us the opposite of the wise man – the foolish man. The foolish is characterized by bitter envying and strife – the lust of the flesh. Certainly James cannot be referring to Christians!?!? He must be talking about lost people! Well, certainly lost people can be characterized as foolish. However, Christians can also be quite foolish (cf. Eph 5:15-17). James is not focusing on the lost; he continues to address Christians. **Christians who are not seeking wisdom are by default seeking foolishness.** They are seeking earthly wisdom which is demonic in nature – influenced by Satan and his entire system.

Christians need to realize the importance of pursuing wisdom! The envy and strife which characterizes many Christian homes and churches is demonic. While Christians cannot be possessed by demons, they certainly can be influenced by demons. This is why it is so important to instead be influenced by the Word. We must let the Word of Christ dwell in us richly (cf. Col 3:16)! We must immerse ourselves in the Word and allow it to conform us to the image of Christ. Our goal should be to know the Word and its great transforming power. If we do not, we will be influenced by the world, flesh, and the devil! There is no sin we are incapable of committing if we are out of step with the Lord. This is what James is saying in verse 16. If we are not walking with the Lord seeking the wisdom proceeding from Him, we are walking in confusion and in the path of sin. We must renounce this practice and seek the Lord. He loves us and wants us to walk in the victory of wisdom!

In verses 17-18, James paints the picture of a Christian who is influenced by heavenly wisdom: this Christian walks in the spirit, they are pure and righteous, they are peacemakers, they are gentle and not overbearing, they are willing to submit to others, they are full of mercy, they are not partial or hypocritical. Wow! Who does that sound like – the Lord Jesus Christ of course! This is the kind of person we should desire to be – holy, just, and loving!

When we are dedicated and committed to following the Lord, seeking the wisdom He promises (cf. 1:5; Prov 2:6), we will be a changed people. Our actions will be seen by others which will produce a great witness. One goal of a wise walk with the Lord is the influence it can have on others. As peace characterizes our lives, others will have hope. Peace is an important facet of the fruit of the Spirit – love.

The thing James' original readers needed was wisdom. We have already seen that some of them had a problem with partiality and hypocrisy. Some did not love the Lord or each other. These are valuable lessons we can learn and apply to our lives. We must seek to be wise men and women! Wisdom that comes from above is none other than the Spirit filled life.

DISCUSSION QUESTIONS AND IDEAS

- Define and describe wisdom.
- Discuss the absolute necessity for seeking to be wise.
- Discuss how being a Christian does not necessarily mean one is wise.
- Reinforce the need for all of us to seek wisdom. Give examples of how foolish choices Christians make can haunt them for life. Conversely, give examples of how wise choices result in blessing.
- Lead a discussion on exactly how Christians can gain wisdom: seeking the Lord through His Word and prayer; saying no to foolish things; choosing to say yes to the right things; making life altering decisions early, rather than later in their life; keeping the pursuit of wisdom at the forefront of our mind every day.

CHAPTER 15
LUST AND WAR

James 4:1-3

¹From whence come wars and fightings among you? come they not hence, even of your lusts [desires] that war in your members? ²Ye lust, and have not: ye kill [murder], and desire [covet] to have, and cannot obtain: ye fight and war, yet ye have not, because ye ask not. ³Ye ask, and receive not, because ye ask amiss, that ye may consume it upon your lusts [pleasures].

Starting with Chapter 4, we begin the last section of James' epistle. Remember, the outline for the main body of the book is found in 1:19, *Wherefore, my beloved brethren, let every man be swift to hear, slow to speak,* **slow to wrath**. Chapter 4 begins the section on being *slow to wrath*. Thus far, James has done a marvelous job of speaking very practically with significant doctrinal emphasis. In other words, James has told us how to live what we believe. More specifically, he has told us how we many times are not living what we believe. In fact, James made sure that we understood in order to live what we believe, we must first know what we believe. We must be *swift to hear* so that we can be *slow to speak* and then *slow to wrath*. Hence, James has a great reverence for the Word of God. He wants us to understand and be wise. This wisdom – the wisdom worth having – originates from God via His Word. If we strive to have this wisdom, our reward will be the *crown of life* (1:12). Let's begin to investigate how we can be *slow to wrath* in 4:1-3.

No doubt James has a loving pastor's heart. One way to tell this is he is not afraid to address difficult issues head on. He will speak directly in this section. He powerfully tells it like it is. Of course, he does so with a heart of love. James fears for the lives of his *brethren* and wants them to change their ways. In this section (4:1-3) he addresses the problem of strife and contention that was evidently a major problem amongst the *brethren*. The *brethren* are members of the *body of Christ*. They are men and women, children, rich, poor, etc. who have received the gift of eternal life by simply believing the Word of God (1:18; John 1:12-13; 3:16-18; 6:47). Thus, James does not address the lost world, rather he speaks with passion and concern to his brothers and sisters in Christ. How we act is very important!

If you remember in Chapter 3, James asked a question in verse thirteen, *Who is a wise man and endued with knowledge among you?* He went on to say a wise man shows his wisdom essentially by walking in the Spirit. The wise man is a peacemaker. Based on the question James poses in 4:1, wisdom was not characteristic of many of the brethren. They were embroiled in strife and contention. It appears they were at war with each other. They had let circumstance get the best of them, and they were fighting from within.

It is sad this was a problem back in the first century among brothers and sisters in Christ. It is equally as sad the same problem exists today. Much of what God wants to do among us is hindered because we quench the Spirit (1 Thes 5:19). To quench the Spirit means to extinguish Him. When we operate in the lust and desires of our own flesh, the power of the Spirit in our lives is stifled. Comparing the Spirit to a fire, it is like taking a bucket of water and pouring it on a warm fire. The Spirit of God is our comforter and guide. He has come to reveal the truths of God to us and to bring us close to the Father. When we are engulfed with war and strife, He is grieved and will not accomplish what He wants to do.

Since we can see the vast importance of not grieving or quenching the Spirit, how do we avoid it? How do saved people avoid walking in the flesh? We will answer these questions in a moment. In 4:1, James tells us in no uncertain terms the problem is within us. We must not look for someone to blame. Even though we have been born again, there is a battle inside us between our old nature and the new nature (cf. Rom 7:23). We should reflect back in Chapter 3 and see envy and self-seeking (3:14) is prevalent among James' readers. Many were in competition with one another to show who was the "wisest" (3:1, 13). Not surprisingly, there was *confusion and every evil work* among them (3:16).

We all know that just because we have been born again we are not yet without sin. Every Christian battles with sin each and every day. How do we win the victory over this battle? James has already told us how to win the victory – through the life saving power of God's Word (1:21). God's Word is our refuge. From it comes wisdom. We must realize, acknowledge, and accept the fact we are in a battle for our lives. The Devil and his system are opposed to us. Knowing this, as soldiers we must prepare for battle each and every day. Our sword being the Word of God and our shield being faith in the revealed will of God (cf. Eph 6:12-17). The psalmist said, *thy word have I hid in my heart that I might not sin against thee.* (Ps 119:11) The answer to how we win the battle is found in an abiding relationship with our Lord Jesus Christ (John 15:7; 1 John 2:28). We must do more than want to know about Him; we must want to *know Him* in a very intimate way (cf. Phil 3:10). Until we as Christians are willing to seek the Lord above all else, we will perpetually lose the battle. We must spend quality time in the Word and on our knees. In many cases, prayer and fasting are necessary (Matt 17:21). If there is a problem we just cannot seem to overcome or a circumstance where we cannot seem to find victory, then we should seriously consider the Biblical answer – prayer and fasting. If we are serious about victory in our Christian life, prayer and fasting will be part of our battle plan. While not a short cut answer, this answer is Biblical.

To go further, if we are seeking to do the will of God, we will be humble peacemakers. If there is strife and contention, we will realize the deadly effects of such. We will seek forgiveness and peace between others. We will be the instigator of forgiveness and peace. We will see to it that the problem is addressed. If we want to win the war between our old and new nature, we must feed the new, starving the old (cf. Eph 4:17-5:21). We must evaluate ourselves in light of Scripture and see how we are doing. We will most assuredly find some area of weakness. As we meditate upon the Word and ask the Lord to help us see what we need to change, our eyes will be focused upon what we need to change rather than on what our wife, husband, children, friends, etc. need to change. In fact, one of the ways to best effect change in others is to change ourselves. When we change, others will see the difference and be more apt to change. Further, as we allow the Word to transform us, humility and meekness will begin to characterize our lives. This is a sign of wisdom. As we become wise, others will want what we have. Hence, the way to minister to others is to yield to God via His revealed will – His Word. The way to minister to others is to allow God to change us first! War and fighting must stop and be replaced by peace and unity.

In verse 2 James says, *Ye lust, and have not: ye kill [murder], and desire [covet] to have, and cannot obtain: ye fight and war, yet ye have not, because ye ask not.* These believers were filled with a lust for power and prestige in some form or fashion. They desired to get ahead of each other in some way. They desired attention or prestige in such a way that they possibly were saying to themselves, 'I wish my brother or sister were dead! Then I would have the power/prestige.' Certainly this type of hateful attitude is not a righteous work. The problem was accentuated when their desire was not fulfilled, which resulted in more fighting and war. While they were not literally committing murder, they were committing murder in a metaphorical sense. John tells us if we hate our brother, we have committed murder (1 John 3:15). Yes, our sinful nature is capable of committing *every evil work* (3:17). That is why we must not war against each other; rather we should be at war with our old nature along with the Devil and his world system. Our battle should be focused in the proper direction! We must be holy warriors fighting the enemy, not those on our side!

James next reveals one reason these believers are not satisfied – they are not asking! In verse 3 James expands the thought by saying, *Ye ask, and receive not, because ye ask amiss, that ye may consume it upon your lusts [pleasures].* James reveals several truths for us while couching them in a very practical setting. Our desires can be met by God! All we must do is ask! God is a loving and giving Father. He wants to give us the desires of our hearts. Notice Jesus' words in the Sermon on the Mount:

> [7]Ask, and it shall be given you; seek, and ye shall find; knock, and it shall be opened unto you: [8]For every one that asketh receiveth; and he that seeketh findeth; and to him that knocketh it shall be opened. [9]Or what man is there of you, whom if his son ask bread, will he give him a stone? [10]Or if he ask a fish, will he give him a serpent? [11]If ye then, being evil, know how to give good gifts unto your children, how much more shall your Father which is in heaven give good things to them that ask him? (Matt 7:7-11)

What we must realize is that our heart must be in the proper place. In order for our Father to give us good gifts, we must want good gifts. If we want evil things, our Father is certainly not going to give them to us. As we allow the Word of God to change our lives, we will begin to desire godly things. Our desire will be in line with God's will. It is then that we can ask and receive. This kind of mind is best observed in Jesus as He sought His Father's will perpetually (John 5: 17-20; 17).

We can have what we want! God's nature is to give and give and give. He is love and love shares. God wants us to have peace and unity. He does not want us to be embroiled in strife and contention. The key to avoiding what our old nature does so naturally is to feed upon the Word of God. When we do so, we will be changed into the person we should be and the one God wants us to be. We will realize a "salvation" that will yield satisfaction beyond our imagination (1 Cor 2:9). We will be saved from the strife and contention of this life receiving the peace and contentment our Father wants for us. As we continue in this way, we will walk in wisdom which, when we stand before our Judge, will yield the *crown of life* – the reward our Father wants us to have!

DISCUSSION QUESTIONS AND IDEAS

- Discuss the danger of strife and contention, especially in a family.
- Discuss how easy it is to fight and be at odds with each other. Explain why it is so easy.
- Talk about the power of the Spirit, yet the ability to quench the Spirit by serving self.
- Ask for reasons why some are involved with strife and contention.
- In light of the battle we face, discuss the answer of Biblical meditation, prayer, and fasting.
- Discuss why we need to change our priorities and desires to match those of God.
- Ask for an example of a battle plan we can have to quench strife and allow the Spirit to burn brightly in our life. Emphasize the absolute need for Biblical meditation, prayer, and fasting. Also, emphasize the need to have intimacy with our Lord....talk about the sweet abiding fellowship we can have with the Creator of the Universe (1 John 1:4)!

CHAPTER 16
WHO'S YOUR FRIEND

James 4:4-6

⁴Ye adulterers and adulteresses, know ye not that the friendship of the world is enmity with God? whosoever therefore will be a friend of the world is the enemy of God. ⁵Do ye think that the scripture saith in vain, The spirit that dwelleth in us lusteth to envy? ⁶But he giveth more grace. Wherefore he saith, God resisteth the proud, but giveth grace unto the humble.

As James continues in this last section on being *slow to wrath*, he forcibly reveals a major shortcoming in the lives of his readers. This shortcoming has been prevalent among God's people throughout history. It is prevalent today among God's people. This shortcoming is a very difficult "pill to swallow." It is spiritual adultery! As we have already observed, James speaks with a heart of compassion and truth. He speaks *the truth in love* (Eph 4:15). Since love *rejoices in the truth* (1 Cor 13:6), it is quite understandable why James addresses this most important matter. He reveals the ramifications of spiritual adultery – enmity with God! Certainly, God's people – Christians – do not really want to be at odds with their Lord! However, James reveals when we are friends of the world, we are enemies of God. He encourages us in this passage to befriend the Lord and receive the grace He wants to bestow upon us. In order for believers to receive this grace, we must humble ourselves.

In verse 4, James does use some very forceful language to describe an unfaithful Christian – an adulterer! James is not speaking of physical adultery, rather spiritual adultery. Of course, the Christian who commits physical adultery is at that very moment also committing spiritual adultery. But James is not focusing on physical adultery; instead he is dealing with the spiritual unfaithfulness of some of his Christian readers. To be sure, physical adultery is defined as being sexually unfaithful to one's spouse. When a man and woman are married, their sexual intimacy is limited to each other. When either partner is unfaithful sexually by having intimate sexual relations with someone other than their spouse, they have committed adultery. While not physical, Jesus also mentioned mental adultery in the Sermon on the Mount (cf. Matt 5:27-28).

Using the readers understanding of physical adultery, James points out their spiritual unfaithfulness. He speaks *the truth in love*. James reveals the state of their misguided lives. He helps them (and us) by pointing out the need to be faithful to our Lord. No doubt, James draws from Old Testament Scripture which refers to Israel being in a covenant relationship with the Lord as Husband and wife (cf. Jer 31:32). It is also well known that Israel committed spiritual adultery (cf. Hos 2:2-5; 3:1-5: 9:1). Using this context, James tells Christians to not be guilty of the same offense. In fact, he states some are doing this very thing.

We must review the fact Christians are being addressed. In order to commit spiritual adultery, one must be related. Since God has birthed the readers from above (cf. 1:18), we know they are in a relationship with the Lord (cf. 2 Cor 11:2). Further, this relationship is all of God's doing. We know this because the Scriptures state *by his own will begot He us* (1:18). John shared the same truth in John 1:13. God is the one who has given us the gift of eternal life, and we have simply been the receivers of this marvelous gracious gift. This gift of eternal life is received by faith alone. Upon receipt, we become children of God in an irrevocable and unending relationship with Him! Since we are indelibly related, our fellowship with the Lord is always the focus for us as believers. Our ongoing fellowship with our Lord is only possible because we have a relationship with Him. Again, the reason we have a relationship is because our Lord chose it to be so – He was the initiator. He loved us first and offered us the free gift of eternal life with the status of children (cf. 1 John 4:19; John 1:12).

Since we are firmly ensconced in the truth of our relationship with the Lord, James can teach us to maintain our fellowship with God. Loving faithfulness is the key to maintaining fellowship with our Lord. He commands us to love Him and our fellow man (cf. Matt 22:34-40; John 13:34). By doing so, we are faithful to Him and can enjoy all the benefits of our relationship with Him. When we are unloving and unfaithful, we will suffer the consequences of our sin. Thank the Lord we can restore fellowship by confessing our sin (cf. 1 John 1:9).

One mark of loving faithfulness is friendship. If we want to be known as the *friend of God* (2:23), we must remain in love with Him. We must trust Him as well as the promises He has made. We must be hearers and doers of the Word (1:25). We must imitate Abraham and Rahab who believed God and were obedient. If we do not, we are not being the *friend of God*. Also, remember we are not looking for the Almighty Lord to be our friend. Rather, we are seeking to be a friend to the Almighty. He is never referred to in Scripture as our friend for He is the Creator and none can approach His status. In no way can we be on the same plane as our Lord.

With this in mind, James tells us if we are spiritually unfaithful, we are not being friendly with God. He tells us our apathy and sin defaults us into being a friend of the world. James uses the Greek word *kosmos* for world. This word is used by James and John to refer to the world system controlled and ruled presently by Satan. Being a friend of Satan means we are more interested in his system than God's. We are more concerned with Satan's domain than God's will. Since Satan is God's enemy, we become God's enemy when we befriend Satan's world. How do we do this? By allowing ourselves to be conformed to the world (cf. Rom 12:2). If our lives are characterized by strife and contention (as was the case among James' readers cf. 4:1-3) we are befriending the world. Satan's system is characterized by this behavior, and he is looking for as many people to befriend Him as possible, especially Christians.

Think of the ramifications of being Satan's friend! How will he treat his friends? Then think of the benefits of being God's friend? How will He treat His friends? The answer is obvious – our loving and gracious Lord is Who we should befriend. He is altogether loving, willing to bestow good gifts we cannot begin to imagine (1:17; 1 Cor 2:9)! Satan wants to rob Christians of everything possible. Since he cannot take our gift of eternal life (cf. John 10:28-29), he works on the next best thing – our eternal reward (cf. Rev 3:11). Yes, while the quantity of our eternal life cannot be affected, our quality or enjoyment of eternal life can be affected. Satan *as a roaring lion, walketh about, seeking whom he may devour* (1 Pet 5:8). He wants to rob us of temporal joy and victory as well as eternal reward. Satan does not want us to receive the *crown of life* (1:12; Rev 3:11). This is the primary reason he energizes his *kosmos* the way he does. He wants to trip up every believer so they live in doubt and despair as opposed to confidence and joy (cf. 1 John 2:28). We must apprehend this simple yet many times evasive truth.

In verse 5, James emphasizes the truth of Exodus 20:5 and 30:14. Since we are God's people – Christians – God is jealous in the proper way. We are in a relationship with Him, where He lovingly and righteously demands faithfulness. We grieve Him and hurt ourselves when we are unfaithful by befriending Satan. God does not want to "share us" for two primary reasons. First, we are His, and He wants uninterrupted intimacy with us. God loves us, and because we have a relationship with Him, He wants us to reciprocate that love. Certainly, *we love Him because He first loved us* (1 John 4:19). Because of this *we ought also to love one another* (1 John 4:11). This simple truth should guide us causing us to see the importance of our love relationship with the Lord. Second, God is jealous over us because He wants for us to experience the best He can give. He knows Satan is a liar and makes promises he cannot deliver. So God is at work but actually grieved when we walk contrary to His love. Just as a man and his wife should love one another and want to protect that special God ordained fellowship, so should Christians do so with the Lord. We should have godly jealously towards our loving Lord. If we are not doing so, we should repent and fall back in love with our wonderful Lord (cf. Rev 2:1-5).

In verse 6, James quotes Proverbs 3:34. He shows God's children that His grace is never exhausted. God is full of grace and mercy, willing to extend it to His children. To experience this grace, we must humble ourselves. If we have strayed away, then we can come back. If we have been a spiritual adulterer, God is willing to forgive and show His grace. Our fellowship can be restored. We simply need to repent of and confess our sins knowing the Lord is *faithful and just to forgive us* of the sin we confess (1 John 1:9). However, His grace is such that not only will He forgive the sin we confess, He also is faithful to forgive any other sin that stands between us! The sacrifice of Jesus is so powerful and effective that it allows God to forgive sin, restoring fellowship with us. This is another aspect of His mercy and grace. As stated above, in order to receive this grace, we must humble ourselves and admit our wrong doing. Pride will cause us to continue in spiritual adultery. This will result in estrangement from our Lord. We will not be able to experience the joy of His fellowship (cf. 1 John 1:4). Oh, that we would listen to the voice of the Lord through James! Grace and mercy are available to us from our Lord.

DISCUSSION QUESTIONS AND IDEAS

- Define adultery and discuss its negative ramifications.
- Discuss spiritual adultery and its negative ramifications.
- Have the group members explain how friendship works.
- Ask why the Lord is jealous over us?
- Discuss the grace of God for humble believers.

Perseverance Pays

CHAPTER 17
HUMILITY'S PATH

James 4:7-10

⁷Submit yourselves therefore to God. Resist the devil, and he will flee from you. ⁸Draw nigh to God, and he will draw nigh to you. Cleanse your hands, ye sinners; and purify your hearts, ye double minded. ⁹Be afflicted, and mourn, and weep: let your laughter be turned to mourning, and your joy to heaviness. ¹⁰Humble yourselves in the sight of the Lord, and he shall lift you up.

If we are going to be *slow to wrath* (1:19), James tells us submission and humility must mark our Christian lives. We are going to need to resist what comes natural to us. The source of what comes natural – sin – originated with the Devil, the original sinner in God's creation. If we will submit ourselves to God in humility, we can then resist the Devil. When we resist the Devil, his efforts will be defeated and victory will be ours. James tells us here that in order for us to do so, we must cleanse ourselves of known sin in our lives. Confession and repentance of sin is difficult but required if we are to walk as victorious Christians who will someday be awarded the *crown of life* (1:12).

The preceding verses in this section were hard hitting and revealed that James' readers were entangled in lust and fightings. Their Christian walk was anything but victorious. The Lord was not pleased with them for certainly they had left their first love. (cf. Rev 2:4) They were going through the motions, but their actions were in their own power – the power of their flesh. As we think back through James' epistle, we see the sin of his readers: not listening to God or obeying His Word, showing partiality, not showing brotherly love, speaking hatefully, envy, strife, quarrels, lust, and friendship with the world (cf. Gal 5:19-21)! Wow, what a list! Does it remind you of anyone today? Do we not all face these very same issues today? Of course, we may be in different circumstances, but we are facing the very same issues.

As believers in Jesus Christ, we have the gift of eternal life as a present possession – it is a gift of God delivered of His grace and received by faith (1:18; John 3:16, 18, 36; Eph 2:8-9). Hence, we have a relationship with God, being His children. As we all know about children, they are not born mature. Children need to grow! So it is in the spiritual realm – babes in Christ need to grow. This growth is where James **focuses** His attention. It is where we need to **focus** our attention also. What comes natural to us is sin – the same sin James describes. In order for us to have victory in our Christian life, we must shun sin and seek first the kingdom of God (cf. Matt 6:33). To seek first the kingdom simply means to seek God's will. His will is for Jesus to return and rule in righteousness. Further, the Father's will is that you and I accompany Jesus as rulers in His kingdom! What an awesome privilege! Paul tells us to *seek those things which are above* in Col 3:1. This is the same thing as seeking the kingdom.

If we seek first the kingdom of God, we will experience joy and fulfillment. God will supply our every need! If we continue to seek the Lord's will, then when we enter that kingdom, we will receive reward and commendation we cannot begin to imagine (cf. 1 Cor 2:9; 2 Pet 1:10-11). By seeking the Lord and His coming kingdom, we are laying up treasures for ourselves in heaven just as our Lord commanded us in Matt 6:19-20! Conversely, if we are overcome by the world, flesh, and Devil, we will experience loss of reward (cf. Matt 25:24-30; 1 Cor 3:15) as well as shame before our Lord (cf. 1 John 2:28). So let's listen to what James has to say realizing the vast importance of his instruction. Much rides on how we conduct ourselves as Christians. Later in 5:9, James reminds each of us *the judge standeth at the door*.

Submission! What a challenging word for us. Maybe submission comes easier for some than others. To submit means to be in **willing** subordination to someone else; it means to obey what someone else says. While everyone practically must be subordinate to someone else, this does not make it appealing to us. As sinners, we are rebels by nature not wanting to submit to anyone. Yes, in certain areas of our lives we find it acceptable to submit, but at our core we are rebels who want to be in control. If we have this fact in mind, we can better understand our battle with the Devil and ourselves. Satan wants to use our very own nature against us. He wants us to trick ourselves into thinking we can be victorious Christians yet not be in submission to God. We must not allow him to deceive us (cf. 2 Cor 2: 11; 11:3, 14)!

Submitting to God, according to James, is simply being a hearer and doer of God's Word (1:25). If we are going to grow and mature in the Lord we must seek Him through much prayer and study. Why is this so difficult for us to do? It is against our nature, that's why. Again, we are rebels who want our own way. We do not want to depend upon anyone else. Remember just because we are God's children does not mean our old nature is gone. It is alive and well. Our battle is to defeat it by the power of our new nature (cf. Eph 4:17-32; Col 3:5-17).

To defeat our sinful nature takes work. This work is our effort which is energized by the Lord (cf. Phil 2:12-13). As we draw close to the Lord, He will draw close to us (4:8). This is what we call merited or earned grace. While some have said grace is defined as unmerited favor, that is not always the case. Certainly, the grace God extended to us for the gift of eternal life is unmerited – we did not work for this grace (cf. Eph 2:8-9; Tit 3:5). However, the grace James mentions in 4:6 and describes further in 4:7-10 is certainly merited. If we want more and different kinds of God's grace, we must submit ourselves to Him. We must obey Him. It is really simple in many respects. The problem that makes things seemingly complicated is how our adversary wants to trick and deceive us from the *simplicity that is in Christ* (2 Cor 11:3). Along with our sinful rebellious nature, Satan is able to lead us down the path of pride rather than the path of humility. If we have any hope of winning the *crown of life* (1:12), we must persevere walking along humility's path.

What does submission to God look like in our Christian life? Well, all of us are different in many respects. We each have different temperaments, backgrounds, and circumstances. However, we are all very much alike in many respects. In general each of us battle our flesh, the Devil, and the world system. If we are going to submit to God, we must do the following: First, we must acknowledge our sinful nature. We must not think we have arrived simply because we have been born again. Second, we must be students of God's Word. It is the *perfect law of liberty* that will deliver us from our sinful ways (1:21, 25). The psalmist said *thy word have I hid in my heart that I might not sin against thee.* (Ps 119:11) Third, we must be prayer warriors (cf. 5:16; Matt 26:41). The strength of our spiritual life is revealed in our prayer life.

All of these things must be done in the spirit of meekness and humility. If we are submissive to God, we will come to Him seeking to know Him on a more intimate level. Simply put, we must be in love with Him! Love is a choice. We define love as having great affection towards someone or to count someone as being precious and of great value. As we ponder our Lord via His precious Word, our love for Him will grow. As we consider His goodness towards us, our affection for Him will increase. As we fall deeper and deeper in love with our Lord, submission will become less of a struggle (cf. Matt 11:28-30). We will become like Jesus who had the most intimate relationship possible with His Father. Our goal is to love the Lord like Jesus loved His Father (cf. John 17). This is all very achievable for us because God is love, desiring loving fellowship with His children (cf. 1 John 1:1-4; 4:7-19). Isn't that awesome?

Ponder for a moment the Creator desiring intimate fellowship with you and me. Think about the condescension Jesus made for us. Consider His present work for us as our High Priest. How much time does He spend pleading our case before the Father! Muse over the reward Jesus wants to provide us for a job well done. Reflect upon the work of the Holy Spirit in our lives and His provision for our needs as well as His guidance for us. If we truly will step back and meditate upon these things (we have just begun to scratch the surface of God's goodness towards us), we will fall much deeper in love with the Lord. Quiet meditation – focused one on one time with the Lord – will allow us to see more clearly the eternal matters. As we meditate upon the Lord, we will begin to see him in His glory and splendor. We will see Him high and lifted up! This will cause us to love Him more and more. It will also cause us to see the extent of our sinfulness!

Confessing our sin is definitely a major part of submitting to God. As we have observed, we are quite capable of any kind of sin. Let's take an Old Testament example of submission. Psalm 51 records David's confession of His adultery with Bathsheba, his lies, and murder of her husband Uriah. Wow! As we think about David's sin, we must comprehend the time line. David, the man after God's heart, was in sin for over a year before approached by Nathan the prophet. God used Nathan to reach David. Undoubtedly, David had rationalized his sin and was living in denial. When the Word of the Lord came through Nathan the prophet, David was convicted by the power of God through His Word. David had not fallen so far away that he had become callous. He probably was struggling with his sin in numerous ways. There is not a person on earth more miserable than a child of God who is out of fellowship with the Lord. The farther and longer we fall away, the more difficult it is for us to come back. All the more reason for us to seek the Lord continually by confessing all known sin while communing with Him early and often.

David's prayer in Psalm 51 is one of confession where he seeks restored fellowship with the Lord. In verse 1, he pleads for God's mercy and forgiveness. Although David had been in a state of sin for over a year, he still knew His Lord was willing to forgive and restore fellowship. David understood the depths of God's love and forgiveness. In verse 2, he desires cleansing from sin.

This cleansing is for renewed fellowship as his relationship was not in question.[1] In verses 3 and 4, David acknowledges and confesses his sin against God. He knows in order to make things right with the Lord, he must come clean. In verse 10, David again wants to be cleansed and thus renewed. His heart (mind, cf. Rom 12:2) has been dirty. He now wants to be cleansed. In verse 12, David desires joy as well as freedom. The salvation God provides for His children involves joy and freedom. David inevitably was unable to experience these benefits while in a state of denial. While embarrassed and humiliated, joy in addition to freedom was restored as he confessed and began again to walk in fellowship with the Lord. This Old Testament example of repentance and confession typifies the need for submission and humility in our lives. David's desire for fellowship with God demanded humility.

Submission to God will result in an ability to resist the Devil. In fact, if we are not submitting to God, we are by default submitting to the Devil! As we submit to God, the Devil will eventually leave us alone. This does not mean he will not return to tempt us again. However, it does mean that we have the ability to experience deliverance (salvation) in our day to day lives. If we submit to God and resist the Devil, we can have a victorious Christian life. As we draw near to God, He will draw near to us as 4:8 assures. Of course, we need to remember our relationship with God does not change. In the sense of relationship, God is as close to us as possible with this closeness never changing. However, relative to fellowship, we can become

---

[1] For a discussion on relationship and fellowship, please see page 53.

estranged from God. As His children, He is willing to restore fellowship with us if we submit to Him. Further, the more we consistently walk with the Lord, the closer we get. The more we love Him the more He will love us (cf. John 14:15, 21, 23). The more He loves us, the more we can then love Him in return. What an awesome experience to be intertwined in a circle of love with the Creator!

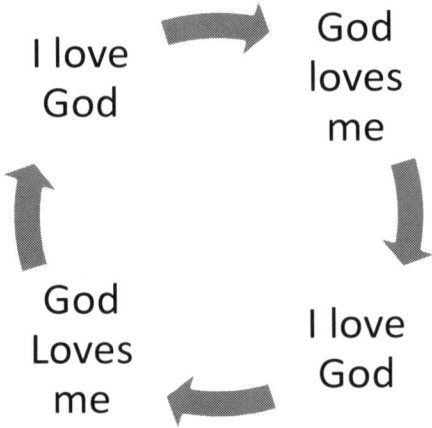

With restoration to fellowship in mind, James describes submission in verses 8 and 9 as confession and contrition. As we evaluate our sinful state and various sinful habits, we should become sorrowful. While we all want to "walk in the victory," we must not forget the times in our lives which require sorrow and contrition. The Apostle Paul realized his sinful state when he referred to himself as the *chief of sinners*. Also, we must remember Jesus did not live on the "mountain" all the time. While He never sinned, He was affected by a sin-filled earth. Consequently, He experienced sorrow (Isa 53:3; Matt 26:38). As we deal with sin in our lives and in the lives of others close to us, we will undoubtedly be sorrowful. We will, just like David, need to be cleansed from our sin. Dealing with sin via repentance and confession is difficult as well as humiliating.

If we have sinned against someone else, we need to ask for forgiveness. If we delay our confession not seeking to restore fellowship with others, our fellowship with the Lord is hindered. We must recognize the Lord can use any situation for our good and His glory. If we are to submit to Him, we must seek to walk in the pathway of humility. Humility is the opposite of pride, haughtiness, and arrogance. God has called us to the pathway of humility. While on this earth our goal is not to elevate ourselves over others. Being humble means we are willing to abase ourselves, thus serving others. The first person we are to serve is God. As we humble ourselves to serve the Lord, we will see that He wants us to serve others. No one illustrated this better than the Lord Jesus Christ. He was obedient to the Father even to the point of death. What did God do for Jesus because of His humility? He gave Jesus a name above every name. Because Jesus humbled Himself on the earth, God rewarded Him with honor and majesty in the heavens (cf. Phil 2:5-11).

The path of humility Jesus walked resulted in His exaltation. In the end, God rewarded Jesus for His obedience. Jesus taught us the secret of greatness was humility (cf. Matt 18:4; 23:12; Luke 14:11). James, an adherent student of Jesus, teaches us the very same thing in verse 10. God will reward us for humbly submitting to Him. Peter declared:

[6] Humble yourselves therefore under the mighty hand of God, that he may exalt you in due time: [7]

Casting all your care upon him; for he careth for you. ⁸ Be sober, be vigilant; because your adversary the devil, as a roaring lion, walketh about, seeking whom he may devour: ⁹ Whom resist stedfast in the faith, knowing that the same afflictions are accomplished in your brethren that are in the world. ¹⁰ But the God of all grace, who hath called us unto his eternal glory by Christ Jesus, after that ye have suffered a while, make you perfect, stablish, strengthen, settle you. (1 Peter 5:6-10)

Yes, humility's path is difficult, but its long term rewards are out of this world! Stay on humility's path. *For God is not unrighteous to forget your work and labour of love.* (Heb 6:10) Stay on this path, for God will reward you in due time. Remember, perseverance pays!

DISCUSSION QUESTIONS AND IDEAS

- Define submission and ask for practical examples of submission.
- Discuss the difficulty we all have with submission.
- Ask who is more admirable, the humble or arrogant person.
- Describe the pathway of humility for believers. Explain how we can become and remain humble as well as submissive to God.
- Discuss the benefits/rewards of being submissive and humbling ourselves.

Perseverance Pays

CHAPTER 18
WATCH WHAT YOU SAY

James 4:11-12

¹¹Speak not evil one of another, brethren. He that speaketh evil of his brother, and judgeth his brother, speaketh evil of the law, and judgeth the law: but if thou judge the law, thou art not a doer of the law, but a judge. ¹²There is one lawgiver, who is able to save and to destroy: who art thou that judgest another?

James continues to help us by speaking very practically. In verses 11 and 12 he essentially tells us to not be fault finders. It is amazing how naturally we are able to criticize others. Our old nature wants to find as many ways to elevate itself as possible. One of those ways is to seek out the bad in others and then magnify their faults. James tells us here to not do this!

Before we examine verses 11 and 12, let's reflect on verse 10 for a moment. It will help us see how James contrasts two extremes. In verse 10, James tells us the secret of greatness – humility. James repeats what the Lord Jesus had taught about greatness and its relationship to humility. Jesus said that if we want to be great, we must be the servant of all (cf. Matt 23:11-12; John 12:24-26). Jesus certainly modeled this role of servant for us while on earth. What an awesome thought to realize the Creator served the created! Even greater, He is still serving as our High

Priest and will continue to serve as King! Yes, God's very nature is love and love must give and serve. While God is certainly high and majestic, He is also lowly and willing to get His hands dirty.

Paul told us about the mindset of Jesus in Philippians Chapter 2. There he tells us we are to love one another just as Jesus did. We are to be servants like Jesus. Because Jesus was an obedient servant, God rewarded Him for His service. The greatness to which the man Jesus attained was a name above every name. Yes, Jesus is God in human flesh: He is the Godman. As a **man** he earned the most elevated position possible. Now angels are subject to Him and soon – in the Father's time – He will return to earth to rule and reign. So the lesson for us to take away from Jesus' words and example is that being obedient to God yields great blessing. God is love, and He wants us to love Him and others by being servants. If we have any other ambition or mindset, we are not set on greatness.

To contrast the path to greatness, James quickly shows the opposite path to insignificance. When we as Christians stray from the narrow path of obedience and submission onto the disobedient path of selfishness, we lose our bearings. We are not thinking clearly nor reflecting upon the clear teaching of Jesus about greatness. If we decide to exalt ourselves here by finding fault with others, we will not experience the greatness God wants for us in His kingdom. We must not forget our goal is to live in such a way that God can say to us "well done." If He says "well done," we can expect the *crown of life* as our reward. With this *crown* we will have achieved greatness! Yes, our perseverance pays big dividends!

But the danger is that we will follow our flesh and lose out on the greatness God has planned for us. We will then be in a position of insignificance. Oh, how sad it would be to stand before our Lord and have to explain why we lived for ourselves instead of for Him.

Realizing what is at stake, let's examine verses 11 and 12 a little closer. When James says *speak not* it can be understood as do not "blab out" against someone else. Many of James' readers were guilty of not showing one another love or consideration. They were not honoring one another nor serving each other. Instead, they were fault finders. They allowed their carnal nature to *bite and devour* one another (Gal 5:15). Again, this kind of behavior comes natural to us even though we have been born again. We must fight valiantly against this carnality by walking in the Spirit (cf. Gal 5).

Fault finding carries a big price. James has a knack for showing the logical conclusion to our actions. We know the law teaches us to love our neighbor. Notice Leviticus 19:18, *Thou shalt not avenge, nor bear any grudge against the children of thy people, but thou shalt love thy neighbour as thyself: I am the LORD*. We also know the Lord Jesus made a special emphasis on loving one another when He said,

> [34]A new commandment I give unto you, That ye love one another; as I have loved you, that ye also love one another. [35]By this shall all men know that ye are my disciples, if ye have love one to another. (John 13:34-35)

To love others is the ultimate commandment given by Jesus. However, when we do not obey this commandment, we are in effect saying it is wrong and of no use. James tells us this when he says the one who speaks evil of his brother is judging the law. Instead of being a doer of the law by loving others, we are judges of the law testifying it is of no importance. We set ourselves at variance with the Supreme Law Giver. Since He alone has the power of life and death, who are we to challenge His authority? James warns us against elevating ourselves to this undesirable position.

So why do we want to be so quick to find fault with others? Primarily because we are insecure. The reason we want to speak evil of others is usually because we want to cover up our own faults. Sometimes we should say good things about others and we do not. This is really just as bad. God wants Christians to see who we are in Christ and be secure. If we realize the blessing we already have in Christ, we will be in a position to serve others and not finding fault. When we are focused on the Lord and His commandment to love, we will speak to others in love, not evil.

Another reason we speak evil of others is we want to become God. Yes, we want to do God's work for Him, especially when someone has provoked us or simply done something wrong to us. We want to take matters into our own hands. We want revenge. We want to be the minister of justice. While there are positions in the world and church that have the authority to administer justice, we must not think we hold these positions on an individual level. We are to turn the other cheek. We are to suffer wrongdoing. We are not to be our own avenger. Paul's edification in Romans is fitting:

> [9]Let love be without dissimulation [hypocrisy]. Abhor that which is evil; cleave to that which is good. [10]Be kindly affectioned one to another with

brotherly love; in honour preferring one another; ^{11}Not slothful in business; fervent in spirit; serving the Lord; ^{12}Rejoicing in hope; patient in tribulation; continuing instant in prayer; ^{13}Distributing to the necessity of saints; given to hospitality. ^{14}Bless them which persecute you: bless, and curse not. ^{15}Rejoice with them that do rejoice, and weep with them that weep. ^{16}Be of the same mind one toward another. Mind not high things, but condescend to men of low estate. Be not wise in your own conceits. ^{17}Recompense to no man evil for evil. Provide things honest in the sight of all men. ^{18}If it be possible, as much as lieth in you, live peaceably with all men. ^{19}Dearly beloved, avenge not yourselves, but rather give place unto wrath: for it is written, Vengeance is mine; I will repay, saith the Lord. ^{20}Therefore if thine enemy hunger, feed him; if he thirst, give him drink: for in so doing thou shalt heap coals of fire on his head. ^{21}Be not overcome of evil, but overcome evil with good. (Rom 12:9-21)

We must realize the severity of our words. We must watch what we say because Jesus said,

^{2}For there is nothing covered, that shall not be revealed; neither hid, that shall not be known. ^{3}Therefore whatsoever ye have spoken in darkness shall be heard in the light; and that which ye have spoken in the ear in closets shall be proclaimed upon the housetops. ⁴And I say unto you my friends, Be not afraid of them that kill the body, and after that have no more that they can do. ⁵But I will forewarn you whom ye shall fear: Fear him, which after he hath killed hath power to cast into hell; yea, I say unto you, fear him. (Luke 12:2-5)

DISCUSSION QUESTIONS AND IDEAS

- Briefly discuss greatness. Give examples of people who were great servants.
- Ask for examples of supposedly great people who ended up not being so great.
- Discuss various ways we can all be servants.
- Talk about the logic James uses concerning judging the law by our fleshly words and actions.
- Discuss Rom 12:21 and what it means to overcome evil with good.

Perseverance Pays

CHAPTER 19
LIFE IS SHORT

James 4:13-17

¹³ Go to [come] now, ye that say, Today or tomorrow we will go into such a city, and continue there a year, and buy and sell, and get gain: ¹⁴ Whereas ye know not what shall be on the morrow. For what is your life? It is even a vapour, that appeareth for a little time, and then vanisheth away. ¹⁵ For that ye ought to say, If the Lord will, we shall live, and do this, or that. ¹⁶ But now ye rejoice in your boastings: all such rejoicing is evil. ¹⁷ Therefore to him that knoweth to do good, and doeth it not, to him it is sin.

James now turns his attention to some believers who do not appreciate the brevity of life. He obviously knows their mentality towards life, thus revealing to them their sinful attitude and actions. He reminds them that their life is like a puff of steam when compared to eternity. We should all stop and think of our short time on earth (75-80 years; maybe 100 years if we are very fortunate) in light of the endless ages. James encourages his readers to live in the present with the future in mind. He obviously has the potential for future blessings in mind as he pens these words. We really cannot comprehend time without end. But James tells us to live for the Lord by always considering His will for our lives. To do otherwise is sin.

Interestingly, verse 13 addresses planning for the future in a somewhat negative light. James summons those who plan for future gain by saying *come now* or *now listen* those of you who decide to go to another city and make money. Certainly, there is nothing wrong with thinking ahead and being proactive. James is not attacking their ambition and forethought. What he is doing is exposing their misguided planning. They are doing so without considering the Lord's plan or will for their lives. They are doing so in the power of their own flesh.

The question arises as to why they would do so? Why would they choose to walk in their flesh and ignore the Lord? Again, these are believers who have experienced the new birth from above (1:18). They are in Christ with a glorious future ahead. They live in a time just after the Lord Jesus visited the earth; they quite probably know people who were eyewitnesses of His resurrection.

Circumstance and time certainly affect our perception of things. These believers were influenced by various difficult issues in life. Remember, they had been scattered from their homeland most likely due to their faith (1:1). Many were looking out for their family's welfare wanting to ensure they had proper provision. Maybe they had become weary and had doubts about the Lord's command to not be anxious regarding daily sustenance (Matt 6:25-34). Or, maybe they had allowed circumstances to cloud their vision, and they were simply focused on gaining riches in the present world without regard for eternal riches (1:12; Matt 6:19-20). Whatever the case, James gets their attention and tells them to listen.

He tells them they do not know what tomorrow holds. What a sobering truth! We do not know what a day can bring.

We are not promised tomorrow (on this earth); we should always be focused on eternity. If we are focused on eternity, we will realize the brief moment we are alive on earth by making it count!

When James says *what is your life*, He is talking about the amount of time we spend on this earth from our natural birth to our natural death. We all know it is a very small blip on the time line of eternity. While we will live forever, the *life* James references is our precursor to eternity. James describes the length of our lives on earth as a puff of steam. Steam quickly dissipates: it is gone, never to return again. While James points out the brevity of our life, he also helps us understand how important it is to make the very most of our time here on earth. Life is short; and we should focus our hearts upon heavenly things. As the psalmist said, *So teach us to number our days, that we may apply our hearts unto wisdom.* (Ps 90:12) Certainly, James is saying we should seek wisdom, for he has mentioned the vast importance of wisdom several times (1:5; 3:13, 17).

The memorable lesson should be that we have but a brief moment on earth to please the Lord. Our time is short; and we should apply ourselves to the most important things. Since we are children of God who have been born again, we should focus all of our attention on pleasing the Lord and seeking His will – His will being for us to persevere and therefore, earn the *crown of life*. If we seek earthly things, we cannot expect to inherit heavenly things. Earthly riches are perishing, but heavenly rewards are eternal (cf. 1 Cor 9:24-27).

James goes on to help us see what a properly focused life is like. The person who is seeking the Lord's will arranges their life accordingly. James has taught us several things about the Lord's will: God has willed that we be born again (1:18); He wants us to endure trials (1:2); the Lord wants us to persevere and win the *crown of life* (1:12); He wants us to love our neighbor (2:8); He desires for us to have mature faith (2:22); our Lord wants us to be wise (3:17); and He desires for us to be submissive and humble in His sight (4:8-10). God's will is not very hard to find. Many times we can overlook the obvious in search for the minutia. God is not a micro manager of our lives as He has allowed us freedom of choice to a certain extent. The secret to knowing the Lord's will even in the smallest areas of our lives can be observed in one word – abiding. As we seek the Lord and grow closer and closer to Him, we will see much more clearly. We will see in the light of eternity. Our choices will become much more clear and focused. The more we know of the Lord and His precepts, the better able we are to walk in His will and way. There really is not a shortcut. We are to abide in Him, and He will guide us (cf. John 15; 1 John 2:28).

James concludes this thought by showing the evil of bragging about earthy plans for success. Those who seek their own desires outside the Lord's will are doing evil. Further, James shows us how those he is addressing know the Lord's will. They know the teaching of Christ concerning reward and responsibility. They know the danger of walking alone and not abiding in the Lord.

James describes the sin of omission. To know to do good and yet not do it is evil. Knowledge is powerful. The principle where much is given much is required is ever present with all of us. The more of the Lord's will we know, the more we are responsible to fulfill His will. Some may say, "I do not want to know any more because I do not want to be responsible." This will not work either, because we already know we should seek more knowledge. If we neglect to seek the Lord in knowledge and wisdom, we are committing sin. God will hold us accountable for what we know and what we should have known, which is sobering on one hand but encouraging on the other. If we seek the Lord, He has promised to give wisdom (1:5). As we get to know Him more, He will give us grace and everything we need to succeed in this life of trials. If we will delight ourselves in the Lord, He will give us the desires of our heart (cf. Ps 37:4). If we live our lives according to His will, He will bless us with good things (cf. Ps 84:11).

As we meditate on James' words, we should evaluate our love for the Lord. We should look at our lives and determine if we are using our limited time wisely. Several questions should help us evaluate if we are living in the Lord's will:

1. How much quality time do we spend in Biblical meditation and prayer?
2. How deeply do we desire to delve into God's Word?
3. Are we satisfied with a cursory knowledge of God and His Word?
4. How much do we tell other people about the Lord?
5. How much do we succumb to temptation?

The more quality (planned and purposeful) time we spend with the Lord, the closer our walk will be with Him. If we abide in Him, we will then be eager to tell others. Further, we will be given more opportunities to share the Lord's presence in our lives with others as we abide deeper in His love. As we draw close to Him, He draws closer and closer to us (4:8). As we abide in Him, we are able to flee temptation. The answers to the above questions will help us determine how effectively we are using the fleeting moment the Lord has graciously given us. Life is short! We have a crown to win! As Jesus said, *hold fast that which thou hast, that no man take thy crown* (Rev 3:11). May we use our short time here wisely for our good and His glory!

DISCUSSION QUESTIONS AND IDEAS

- Discuss the brevity of our life on earth.
- Give examples of God's will for our lives.
- Explain how we can be sure we are making the most of our time on earth.
- Explore and discuss the good habits one should have which assure us of a successful time on earth.
- Discuss the 5 evaluation questions on being in God's will.

Perseverance Pays

CHAPTER 20
THE DECEIT OF WEALTH

James 5:1-6

¹ Go to [come] now, ye rich men, weep and howl for your miseries that shall come upon you. ² Your riches are corrupted, and your garments are moth-eaten. ³ Your gold and silver is cankered; and the rust of them shall be a witness against you, and shall eat your flesh as it were fire. Ye have heaped treasure together for the last days. ⁴ Behold, the hire of the labourers who have reaped down your fields, which is of you kept back by fraud, crieth: and the cries of them which have reaped are entered into the ears of the Lord of sabaoth. ⁵ Ye have lived in pleasure on the earth, and been wanton; ye have nourished your hearts, as in a day of slaughter. ⁶ Ye have condemned and killed the just; and he doth not resist you.

    With the voice of a prophet, James amplifies his message of truth. While speaking in love, James is not afraid to speak the truth. Make no mistake; love rejoices in the truth (1 Cor 13:6)! Love also speaks woe and warning. James declares the truth about the deceit of wealth. He explains in eschatological language the fate of unrighteous behavior. He reveals the fleeting nature of the present world's wealth. Living the "good life" at someone else's expense is a recipe for judgment. While the rich may think they have gotten away with their unrighteous deeds, they have not. Just because the oppressed do not rise up against their oppressors does not mean the "Heavenly Sheriff" will not ultimately show up. Let's look more closely at what James so powerfully says in this passage.

James' primary audience throughout the epistle is the believer. This is evidenced by his numerous appeals to the *brethren* (1:2, 19; 2:1, 5, 14; 3:1) as well as the instructional nature of the letter. However, in this portion he opens up his message to both Christians and unbelievers. Either can be rich and both can mistreat others because of their riches. Judgment is coming for all people (believer or unbeliever) based on their works. Repentance from sinful works is extremely important for every person. God is not pleased with unrighteousness and has commanded everyone to repent from their evil deeds (Acts 17:30).

The Scriptures do not condemn wealth per se. In 1 Tim 6:17-19, Paul instructs believers who are rich in this world to be willing and ready to help and serve others. The rich believer of this world can also be rich in the world to come by properly using what God has allowed them to have.

The possession of wealth is not sin nor is it wrong to increase one's wealth. Rather, the love of money is declared to be the root of all kinds of evil (1 Tim 6:10). Many of God's servants in Scripture were wealthy: Job, Jacob, David, and Solomon to name a few. However, the Scriptures warn us of the danger and deceit of temporal wealth. Wealth can skew our perception of God and reality. It can also skew our view of ourselves and others. Wealth can cause us to think as well as act contrary to Gods' will. It is this fact we must keep in mind – earthly temporal wealth can deceive any of us! We must not be deceived or have our priorities out of place. We must remember the wealth we should seek is eternal (Matt 6:19-20)! The way to earn this eternal wealth is through perseverance in the faith. A *crown of life* awaits us if we have endured by faith (1:12; 2 Tim 4:6-8).

In 5:1, James thunderously tells the rich men to weep. His context is yet future. Those who are rich should look forward in time and realize they are in for misery. James is certainly focusing upon the return of his half brother the Lord Jesus Christ to establish His kingdom. For it is when the Lord comes that all unrighteousness will be judged. For the rich who have abused their wealth, certain harsh judgment is in store. His tone is not unlike that of Amos when he declared:

> [4] Hear this, O ye that swallow up the needy, even to make the poor of the land to fail, [5] Saying, When will the new moon be gone, that we may sell corn? and the sabbath, that we may set forth wheat, making the ephah small, and the shekel great, and falsifying the balances by deceit? [6] That we may buy the poor for silver, and the needy for a pair of shoes; *yea*, and sell the refuse of the wheat? [7] The LORD hath sworn by the excellency of Jacob, Surely I will never forget any of their works. (Amos 8:4-7)

The material possessions of this world are fleeting. They are not eternal or lasting. Knowing our life is short (4:14) should help us grasp this fact, especially those of us who are blessed with material possessions.

James 5:2 warns that the wealth of many rich people is corrupt and moth-eaten. He uses this language to show how the rich have either obtained or held their riches in an unrighteous manner. This should be contrasted with Jesus' admonition to his disciples for them to store up eternal treasures (Matt 6:19-20). Christians should focus their attention on building heavenly treasures instead of earthly ones. While it is not wrong or against God's will for us to have earthly wealth, we must keep things in perspective. The people James addresses here do not have the proper perspective. Notice his words in 5:3 where he says their precious metals are *cankered*. *Cankered* means rusted and can also mean poisoned. He is telling us our earthly wealth can become corrupt. Having the wealth is not the problem; how it is obtained and managed is the issue.

The Lord is a precious metals inspector and knows corruption when He sees it. James says the corruption will be a witness against the unrighteous rich at the Day of Judgment. This Day of Judgment for the Christian is very real and should be on the top of our mind. It is yet future referred to as the Judgment Seat of Christ (Rom 14:10-12; 1 Cor 3:12-15; 2 Cor 5:8-11). Our works will be evaluated by our Lord to determine their eternal worth. If we have tarnished, corrupt, and rusty works, we will not please Him, therefore not receiving the reward intended for us. Shame (1 John 2:28) and loss of inheritance (Eph 5:5; Col 3:23-25) will be our fate. This reality should cause us to seek Him in love and fear. The unbeliever will also face judgment for his works at the Great White Throne Judgment (Rev 20:11-15). While an unbeliever is doomed to the Lake of Fire for eternity, the severity of punishment will be determined by his works. For more detail on the various judgments of God, see the Summary of Judgments chart in the back of this book.

In 5:4, James reveals the trajectory of the cries from the poor. They have risen to the Lord, the Righteous Judge. Those who work for the rich have been mistreated. With money comes power and then the opposite is true – with poverty minimal influence is the norm. But God is for the underdog! He is righteous and will not allow injustice. The rich have committed fraud, and they will not get away with such actions. Nothing escapes the all hearing ear and all seeing eye of the *Lord of Sabaoth* (Lord of Hosts or Armies). *Vengeance is mine, I will repay* (Rom 12:19) is the declaration of Scripture. Rest assured, God will right the wrongs administering holy justice at His return.

Pleasure and ease have characterized the life of the rich in 5:5-6. This has been at the expense of the poor. The poor are essentially defenseless and do not rebel. These poor who refuse to rebel are in the will of God. By faith they know their poverty is temporal. God has chosen the poor who love and obey Him to be owners in His coming kingdom (2:5). Yes, the Lord is for the poor of this world (especially those poor who are His children 1:18) and will make them rich in the world to come. While they may suffer now, joy will be theirs in the future (cf. Matt 5:3-12).

This passage is most intriguing. Many lessons are available from James' moment of prophetic declaration against the rich. Let's ponder a few of the manifold lessons.

Firstly, being rich or of means is not a sin. Nowhere does James or any other passage of Scripture tell us so. However, wealth can be very misleading and dangerous for us. Riches have the uncanny ability to make us self-focused and thus ignore or neglect God's will. Wealth can cause us to not realize how short our lives really are. We can get caught up in material possessions.

Secondly, wealth can mislead Christians into thinking we are blessed of God. Our society leads us to equate God's blessing with material possessions. Many times we attribute things to God that are not attributable to Him. Some being wealth, success, and power. Those among us who "have done well for themselves" are many times declared to be blessed of God. This idea then causes the rich Christian to perceive the blessing of God in their life for the wrong reason. This misperception can then lead to the building up of their fleshly nature. They can adopt an entitlement attitude and a superiority complex. They can also deceive themselves into thinking they are worthy of special privileges (cf. 2:1-5).

Thirdly, we realize the deception the world, our flesh, and the Devil can bring. Our defense against this deception is to seek the Lord. We must humble ourselves and draw close to the Lord (4:8-10). When we are obedient and wise as James prescribes, we will enjoy the manifold blessings of God! James 4:10 tells us *Humble yourselves in the sight of the Lord, and he shall lift you up.*

The truths of God's Word are precious. He wants us to be rich but in the proper time and place. Our walk of faith during our relatively short term on earth is our "investment time" for eternity. God has promised exaltation in the future for the one who humbles himself in the present (4:10; 1 Pet 5:6). In order to be rich, we must first be poor. What a promise – perseverance certainly pays!

DISCUSSION QUESTIONS AND IDEAS

- Discuss the dangers of being wealthy.
- Discuss what it means to be wealthy...who is wealthy and who is not.
- Explain what God commands the wealthy Christian to do.
- Talk about how it is counter-intuitive for the poor to not rebel against the rich.
- Explain the reward for remaining faithful to the Lord in the midst of oppression.

Perseverance Pays

CHAPTER 21
THE LORD IS COMING

James 5:7-8

⁷Be patient therefore, brethren, unto the coming of the Lord. Behold, the husbandman waiteth for the precious fruit of the earth, and hath long patience for it, until he receive the early and latter rain. ⁸ Be ye also patient; stablish your hearts: for the coming of the Lord draweth nigh.

With the body of the epistle complete, James begins his epilogue with verse 7. The various trials Christians face will come to an end. The Lord has promised to return and bring a consummation to human history. As he concludes his letter, James emphasizes his central message of perseverance by commanding patience. He refers to patience three times in verses 7 and 8. With the example of a farmer patiently waiting for his precious crop, James encourages us to have the same mindset. Trials will come and go. Each trial has the express purpose of maturing us. But we must be firmly established in the truth of our Lord's imminent return. There is great reason to be patiently awaiting our Lord's return, for He is bringing His reward with Him (Rev 22:12)!

Scripture ultimately has the future in mind. The focus of Scripture is on the future. Sure, we know the past is addressed, but the future is the burden of Scripture. Further, the coming kingdom of Christ is the grand central theme of Scripture. Jesus' coming kingdom is given much attention, for in that kingdom the concluding purpose of Christ's redeeming work will be completed (cf. 1 Cor 15:25). Jesus spoke of his return and kingdom quite often, especially in Matthew, Mark, and Luke (cf. Matt 16:24-28, 24-25; Mark 1:15; 4:11; 13; Luke 21; 22:28-30). His return to establish His kingdom permeates the Old as well as the New Testament. It is really no surprise that it is at the forefront of James' mind as he pens these words. You see, the kingdom is where the Father's will is consummated (cf. Matt 6:10). The kingdom is where the Son of Man will rule and reign in righteousness. It will be the place of reward for the faithful soldiers of the Cross (cf. 2 Tim 2:3-5). The kingdom is the *rest* to which we are appointed (cf. Heb 4:9). Our best day is yet to come in that kingdom! God, out of His great mercy and marvelous grace, designed it so!

The most comprehensive treatment by Jesus concerning eschatological events (end time events) is found in Matthew Chapters 24 and 25. In these chapters Jesus reveals great truths about His coming and the end of the age. This portion of Scripture deals with the following subjects: the rapture, rewards, judgment, the Day of the Lord, the tribulation, the millennial kingdom, the future for the body of Christ (the Church), the future for the nation of Israel, and the future for the Gentile nations. All these subjects and more are addressed by Jesus in this very famous and critical passage.

No doubt, James has in mind Jesus' teaching concerning eschatological events as he mentions the coming of the Lord twice in these two verses. We will focus our attention on two eschatological truths taught by Jesus.

Firstly, the rapture will occur prior to Christ's return to set up His kingdom. The rapture will begin a chain of events culminating in the physical return of Jesus to the earth to set up His holy kingdom. The rapture is an imminent event. This means it could happen at any moment. Jesus declared no man could know the timing of the rapture (Matt 24:36-42). There are no other events that must occur in order for the rapture to take place. The rapture has no signs! It begins our Lord's Second Advent along with a variety of other end time judgments.[1]

The rapture, while a momentous event and one in which we should all take great comfort, is a summons for judgment. The Judgment Seat of Christ will take place immediately following the rapture. Judgment is a primary purpose for the rapture. God, in His wisdom, has determined to bless the faithful members of the *body of Christ*. So when James mentions the coming of the Lord, he is telling us to first expect the rapture. In looking to the rapture, we also must realize judgment will occur for each and every Christian. This judgment will not determine our eternal fate. Rather, it will determine our eternal reward. This is the time when the *crown of life* will be awarded to the saint who has persevered. Paul described this joyous award in 2 Tim 4:6-8.

Secondly, the kingdom of Christ will be the place of reward for all of God's people. Our discussion of reward will focus upon

---

[1] See the Summary of Major Judgments chart at the end of this book.

the *body of Christ* – those who have believed in Jesus for eternal life and are thus born again (1:18). The *body of Christ* is made up of all nationalities, Jew and Gentile. James' readers, while Jewish by physical birth, were members of the *body of Christ* by spiritual birth. As members of the body of Christ, they were promised reward for perseverance. We too are members of the *body of Christ* since we have believed in Jesus for eternal life. The promises James and Jesus present are most certainly made to us.

James introduced this subject of reward at the beginning of his letter when he promised the *crown of life* for the one who endured trials. God knows we are robed in flesh, but He has decided to reward us for faithfulness to Him. This glorious promise of reward is an immense motivation for us to keep on keeping on. God has, out of His gracious wisdom, chosen the motivation of reward to help us attain greatness. It is greatness God wants for us – regality in Christ's coming kingdom – and it should be what we also desire. We must believe God is *a rewarder of them that diligently seek Him* (Heb 11:6). Believing in Jesus' teaching, James repeats Jesus' doctrine of reward. He emphasizes the great importance of realizing the reward God has prepared for us. It is reward we are to work for in this life (cf. Matt 6:19-20; 1 Cor 9:24-27; Phil 3:11-14; 2 Tim 4:6-8). Our enjoyment of eternal life throughout the ages will be determined to a great extent by our actions in the present. This great teaching spurred James' beginning and concluding words.

With this prophetic motivator in mind, James tells us to be patient. His original words were intended for those who were suffering wrongfully at the hands of the rich. The promise for those who are *patient* is that the Lord will return. He will reward them for their perseverance. He will put down all unrighteousness. Righteously, He will give riches to the poor who are rich in faith and love Him (2:5).

Patience is a manifestation of the work of the Spirit in our lives (Gal 5:22-23). The word for *patience* in verse 7 is a compound word which means to be long tempered. It carries the idea that we should not lose heart. Our focus should be on the final outcome of our life. The race we are running is one towards reward. Therefore, we must persevere in order to win the promised *crown* (cf. 1 Cor 9:24-27). We do this by following Jesus' example. He was reviled and abused but did not vindicate Himself. Rather, he suffered. Because of His obedience to the Father, He was given the reward of a name above every name. All authority has been placed under Him. The **man** Jesus Christ has won the battle, and the Father bestowed upon Him the right to rule (cf. Phil 2:5-11; Heb 1:13; 2:8-9)!

How are we to possess patience? As the world throws various temptations at us while the Lord allows multiple trials in our lives, how can we be patient? The short answer is to be *filled with the Spirit* (Eph 5:18). To be *filled with the Spirit* is to also be filled with the Word of God (Col 3:16). As we are filled with the Word, we can have patience. However, it is not necessarily easy. It takes our diligence and commitment. We must humbly accept that God has appointed us to suffer for a while (1 Pet 5:10). Our suffering will produce *patience* as James tells us in 1:4. Hence, the trials we face are designed by God to mature us and build *patience* in our souls (Luke 21:19). They bring us blessing, and we should view them as such. We are to patiently await the Lord as James 5:7 instructs. We can do this because of the knowledge we have concerning His return. We know (by faith) He will straighten things out. He will take care of all injustice. He will not forget our trials. He will not forget our *labor of love* (Heb 6:10). Out of His abundant riches, He will reward our perseverance (cf. Heb 10:35-36)! With these truths in mind, there are several questions we should ask ourselves: are we patiently awaiting His return? Are we enduring the trials of life with grace and dignity? Or are we grumbling and complaining every step of the way? If the latter is our answer, we should immediately repent and seek the wisdom trials bring.

James invites us to consider the farmer – a prime example of *patience*. The farmer who sows seed in his field expects a precious fruit. He waits patiently for it to come. He knows that in order for the precious fruit to develop, it will take time. He also knows rain is required. Jumping up and down, doing rain dances, or expecting an immediate result is foolish. We must take this example and draw the parallels James intends. God wants us to reap the precious fruit of reward. In order to do so, we must realize and except God's way. It is one that takes time and our diligence. We must establish our hearts in this truth. The Lord is coming, and He could come at any moment – His coming draws near. He wants to say *well done* to us and pay us for our perseverance. We must *abide in Him,* then we can expect a *full reward* (cf. 1 John 2:28; 2 John 8).

DISCUSSION QUESTIONS AND IDEAS

- Discuss the importance of knowing about end time events.
- Discuss the rapture and its main purpose.
- Talk about the meaning of imminence.
- Explain the importance of being ready for the Lord's return.
- Discuss the relationship between being filled with the Spirit and having patience.

Perseverance Pays

CHAPTER 22
THE JUDGE KNOWS ALL

James 5:9-11

⁹*Grudge not one against another, brethren, lest ye be condemned: behold, the judge standeth before the door.* ¹⁰ *Take, my brethren, the prophets, who have spoken in the name of the Lord, for an example of suffering affliction, and of patience.* ¹¹ *Behold, we count them happy which endure. Ye have heard of the patience of Job, and have seen the end of the Lord; that the Lord is very pitiful, and of tender mercy.*

James continues his concluding remarks with practical advice and warning. Focused on upcoming judgment for Christians, James tells us to take heed. Our loving Lord Jesus will judge our actions. One day He will stand in judgment over all of us. However, we should be encouraged because many before us have endured with *patience*. The *patience* of Job is a grand picture of perseverance and the blessing it brings. The Lord is very gracious and giving towards those who obey Him. Because this is so, we should arrange our lives accordingly. We can persevere and thus obtain the mercy intended for us. However, it requires our attention and diligence. Our proper attitude towards the trials of life will yield *patience* as well as a positive outcome on our judgment day. By faith, we can succeed!

Drawing attention to judgment, James warns how the judge stands before the door. This is definitely a warning to his *brethren* as James tells them to behave properly and not *grudge* one another. The word *grudge* could be translated "grumble." The idea behind this word is that we not groan or sigh, especially against our brothers and sisters in Christ. We all are wrapped in flesh and still retain a sinful disposition. Isn't it amazing how powerful our flesh can be? Its influence must not be underestimated. This is the reason for James' continued admonitions. The readers of this letter had attitude problems for sure. They were at times unloving (2:10), unwise (3:13-15), and ungodly (4:4). Like some Christians, they allowed their fleshly passions to rule them. The battle each and every Christian faces is a battle against our old nature. The new nature we possess in our spirit is at battle with our fleshly nature (Gal 5:17). This battle ground is located in our soul (cf. 1 Pet 2:11).

When things go wrong or the circumstances are not to our liking, our natural fleshly reaction is to complain. When at odds with a brother in Christ, what should our reaction be? Should we grumble, complain, and murmur even if we are in the right? No, we must obey God and interact with our brother in love. We certainly should speak the truth, but we should make sure it is in love (cf. Eph 4:15). Sometimes, we should just say nothing. Remember Jesus' directive to be peacemakers and the benefits a peacemaker will enjoy (Matt 5:9). Jesus said the peacemakers would be called the *sons of God*. To be called a *son of God* is an earned regal title – a position of authority. It is a reward for obedience. It should be distinguished from the title *children of God* (John 1:12) which is given freely as a result of simply trusting Christ for the gift of eternal life.

The Judge Knows All

Jesus revealed in John 5:22 that the Father had appointed Him the Judge of all. Thus, all of creation will be judged by the Lord Jesus Christ. Jesus is God, and as such His very essence is love (cf. 1 John 4:10). While His very character is love, He is also holy and righteous (cf. 1 Pet 1:16). Both of these characteristics of God are in complete harmony. For love is holy and pure rejoicing in the truth (cf. 1 Cor 13:4-7). Thus, our holy Lord must act in accordance with His character which demands love and justice. He must judge the actions of every creature.

Because of man's plunge into sin in the garden, condemnation fell from God. Because of Jesus' supreme sacrifice, this condemnation has been lifted from all those who believe. Hence, the judge actually took the judgment for our sin making eternal life possible for every human. But what of our sinful actions after we have received the free gift of eternal life? Can we sin with amnesty? Are we able to get away with sin as a Christian? No, and James helps us see this truth. While our relationship with God was permanently established the moment we believed Jesus for the gift of eternal life, our fellowship with God was not. Therefore, the quality of our relationship varies based on our actions. Further, our actions have eternal ramifications. What we do with our lives as Christians affects our eternal rewards in the coming kingdom. It is this fact we must grasp! We must comprehend the enormity of reward. We must see things as did James and the other apostles. They saw and understood the immense blessing God will dispense to the faithful follower. They also understood the great loss unfaithfulness would produce. Peter encouraged believers to live Spirit filled lives in order that they might have abundance in the kingdom (2 Pet 1:3-11). He went on to say he was an eyewitness to the majesty of Christ in His kingdom while on the mount of transfiguration (cf. Matt 17:1-5). Peter did not want any Christian to miss the abundance God would give as a result of a life lived in obedience and love. Notice Paul's words in the following three passages regarding the judgment Christians will face:

> [12] Now if any man build upon this foundation gold, silver, precious stones, wood, hay, stubble; [13] Every man's work shall be made manifest: for the day shall declare it, because it shall be revealed by fire; and the fire shall try every man's work of what sort it is. [14] If any man's work abide which he hath built thereupon, he shall receive a reward. [15] If any man's work shall be burned, he shall suffer loss: but he himself shall be saved; yet so as by fire. (1 Corinthians 3:12-15)

> [8] We are confident, *I say*, and willing rather to be absent from the body, and to be present with the Lord. [9] Wherefore we labour, that, whether present or absent, we may be accepted of him. [10] For we must all appear before the judgment seat of Christ; that every one may receive the things *done* in *his* body, according to that he hath done, whether *it be* good or bad. [11] Knowing therefore the terror of the Lord, we persuade men; but we are made manifest unto God; and I trust also are made manifest in your consciences. (2 Corinthians 5:8-11)

> [10] But why dost thou judge thy brother? or why dost thou set at nought thy brother? for we shall all stand before the judgment seat of Christ. [11] For it is written, *As* I live, saith the Lord, every knee shall bow to me, and every tongue shall confess to God. [12] So then every one of us shall give account of himself to God. (Romans 14:10-12)

Paul, James, and John all received their teaching on judgment and reward from the Lord Jesus Christ. Jesus gave numerous examples of how He would judge believers. The most revealing is in Matt 25:14-30, the parable of the talents. This parable shows us the fate of the faithful as well as the unfaithful believer. Great reward awaits the faithful; great loss awaits the unfaithful.

Jesus taught his disciples if they would not forgive each other, their Father would not forgive them (Matt 6:14-15; 18:34-35). He also taught every idle word would come under judgment (Matt 12:36-37). Obviously, Jesus was not teaching we could lose the gift of eternal life with these statements. What He was saying is we can lose our eternal reward based on our actions. Actions generated by the flesh will be judged negatively (cf. Col 3:25). Thankfully, we can judge ourselves now (cf. 1 Cor 10:31) avoiding God's judgment in the future. We can repent, asking for forgiveness, and God will forgive. Fellowship can be restored and reward can be retained or gained. Obedience and love for the Lord will result in great blessing and joy.

The sobering truth is that we will be judged for our actions! Because of this fact, we should take heed making wise changes in every area of our lives! As Paul said in Ephesians 4 and

Colossians 3, put off the *old man* and put on the *new man*. We must diligently seek the Lord via meditation and prayer. By doing so we can have patience to endure the trials of this life. As we grow closer to Him, the trials will be more bearable. Our patience will increase performing its *perfect work*. This *perfect work* is a believer who is wise and able to endure more and greater trials.

While judgment is a sobering thought, we must be careful to not get this truth out of balance. As James explains, God is merciful and will make a way for us to escape judgment if we will obey Him. He has given us everything we need to succeed and hear *well done*. We should never be discouraged because of our impending judgment. Rather, we should realize God is for us. He wants to reward us greatly. Thus, His great love drives Him.

The fact of judgment should propel us to live lives pleasing to God. The lives of the prophets serve as an example for us. As we consider all the prophets, one comes to mind who suffered many wrongs and difficult circumstances, Daniel. Daniel was unique in his sufferings. He was diligent to follow the Lord and seek wisdom. Daniel was a man of fasting, meditation, and prayer. How did he endure the lion's den? By a mature trust in God; by a close walk with the Lord; by meditation upon the Scripture; and by an intense prayer life. How can we be like Daniel? By following his example, just as James invites us to do.

Job stands above all in Scripture as an example of patience. Job was certainly afflicted with trials and suffering. Every material blessing he had was stripped away, even His family! However, Job's faith in God's promises was not vanquished. Job struggled with many questions, but he remained faithful to the Lord.

What was the end result of Job's trial? God returned to Job twice the amount of material blessings he previously held. Job was faithful amidst trial, and God did not forget Job's actions. Just as Job enjoyed reward from God, so can we. Hebrews 6:10 reminds us that *God is not unrighteous.* He will not forget our *labor of love.* He will reward us for our patient endurance (Heb 10:35-36). In other words, perseverance pays!

Jesus told his disciples they would be rewarded as rulers over Israel in His coming kingdom because they had forsaken all and followed Him (Matt 19:27-28). Jesus went on to say that anyone who followed in their footsteps would receive 100 fold. This is 10,000 % interest – quite a return on investment!

The glorious truth of judgment and reward permeates the Scriptures. The fact God wants to reward us richly is skillfully and amply expounded in almost every book of the New Testament. We should heed the encouraging yet sobering words of the Apostle John: *And now, little children, abide in him; that, when he shall appear, we may have confidence, and not be ashamed before him at his coming.* (1 John 2:28)

Our Judge, the Lord Jesus Christ, knows all. His all-seeing eyes and all-hearing ears will bring every action under judgment. The good news is He has made provision for us to pass His judgment with flying colors. May we be diligent to hear the all knowing judge say *well done, thou good and faithful servant..... enter into the joy of thy Lord* (Matt 25:21).

DISCUSSION QUESTIONS AND IDEAS

- Discuss Jesus' current role as High Priest in contrast to His coming role as Judge.
- Explain why Jesus is going to judge Christians.
- Discuss ways we can be ready for our judgment day.
- Ponder God's love and wisdom in providing the motivation of reward.

CHAPTER 23
MANIPULATION

James 5:12

¹² But above all things, my brethren, swear not, neither by heaven, neither by the earth, neither by any other oath: but let your yea be yea; and your nay, nay; lest ye fall into condemnation.

Does this verse seem to be inserted at a strange place? After all, it is part of James' final comments. What would swearing have to do with these believers? Why would James say *above all things*....do not swear? What exactly does it mean to swear or take an oath? Let's examine this important passage and see how James is telling us to avoid manipulation, especially of God, at all costs.

Please remember the practicality of James. He has shown us how to navigate the trials and difficulties of this life victoriously. Trials are to be expected, and we are to rejoice because of them (1:2). This straight shooting, tell it like it is language from James, is much appreciated. He goes on to tell us the purpose of trials is to produce maturity (1:4). In 5:9 He warns us to not hold grudges because our Judge is watching and observing our actions. Our studies thus far have revealed numerous warnings, admonitions, and encouragements from

James. We now come to what James felt was very important – to avoid swearing by God's name. By swearing he does not mean using foul language as some suppose. Rather, swearing means to vow, promise, or pledge. It usually involves taking an oath. The essence of swearing is to affirm yourself. When you do so, you are trying to convince someone you are telling the truth. Telling the truth is certainly admirable. Trying to make sure someone believes you is in and of itself not at all wrong. In fact, we know God swore by His own name to affirm the truthfulness of His Word (cf. Heb 3:18; 6:13).

As we learned in the introduction, James referred quite extensively to the Sermon on the Mount. This passage (5:12) is reflective of Jesus' teaching in that sermon (Matt 5:33-37). The essence of Jesus teaching on swearing was that we should be honest and truthful, not needing to swear by heaven to affirm ourselves. To be true, Jesus did not say we could not swear or take oaths like in a courtroom. Rather, He taught we should not swear invoking God's character in our testimony. In other words, we should not attempt to seek self-affirmation by appealing to heaven (God) as our witness. To do so is to take advantage of Him and take His name in vain.

How was this a problem for James' readers? Better yet, how could swearing be a problem for us today? How likely is it for us to take the Lord's name in vain? Again, we are not talking about profanity or vulgar language. We are talking about believers using God to prove a point or get a leg up. Manipulation, using God as leverage, is a serious thing. Bringing God into a situation only to swear by His name is not necessary and is forbidden by Moses, Jesus, and James. We should never try to prove our point by attempting to "put" God on our side. Our answers and points should be simple and straight forward. When we have a disagreement with someone or do not see things the same way, we must leave God out of our attempt for self-justification. This does not mean we do not base our lives or our answers and arguments on God's Word. However, it does mean we should not say things God has not said. It means we should avoid defending our actions attempting to use God as our vindicator. God will vindicate and we should allow Him to do so in His own time.

How might this manipulation be seen today? One illustration could be drawn between the rich and the poor. A rich or well to do believer could certainly feel self-righteous saying God was on his side as evidenced by his wealth, good fortune, and general way of life. He could in essence condemn a poor believer saying the poor believer was obviously in sin because he was not blessed. The poor would feel more abased because the rich had evoked God's blessing upon himself. This actually happens quite often with health and wealth preachers. They believe God has shown them His will is for all believers to be rich and healthy. They presume upon God, saying things God has not said. Doing so, they bring condemnation upon themselves. They spread a false message which leads many astray.

God is certainly not pleased when we attempt to manipulate others using Him to do so. The problem is we want to be in the right many times seeking self-exaltation. We want to prove others wrong and can very quickly attempt to prove God is on our side. The moment we do so, we are manipulating in God's name.

Another way we can manipulate God is to show others how our "results" are God approved. We do not need to seek the approval of others by explaining how God's hand of blessing must be upon our "ministry." "Success" in ministry is not always a sign of God's approval. Many times a big church can feel they are more significant than a smaller church. The big church seems to be doing more for God, and His hand is presumed to be upon it. While this may be the case, it is certainly not a reason to assume God's hand is not upon the smaller ministry. God will judge each person in His own time as Paul reminded in 1 Cor 4:3-5. We must always be mindful of God's Word, not assuming things that may be hidden during the present.

    What should we do? Walk humbly with our God. If we do so, others will see the fruit of such a walk. We will not attempt to unduly affirm ourselves in the sight of others. Our righteous walk will speak for itself. Not seeking affirmation in the midst of differences between other believers shows we are loving and humble. A sure sign of maturity in our lives exists when we are able to wait for vindication. While we may be right, we do not need to beat each other up with "our truth." We must speak truth in love (Eph 4:15). When we humble ourselves, it is pleasing to God. When we are peacemakers, He is pleased. When we are meek, He takes notice of us. His pleasure will be for our good. He has promised to exalt us **after** we humble ourselves (4:10). His pleasure will ultimately result in our pleasure! What a great God we serve! Love, patience, and perseverance will result in great reward!

DISCUSSION QUESTIONS AND IDEAS

- What does it mean to swear?
- Why would God need to swear?
- How can we be guilty of manipulating God?
- How can we avoid the trap of exalting ourselves?

Perseverance Pays

CHAPTER 24
THE POWER OF PRAYER
AND PRAISE

James 5:13-18

¹³ Is any among you afflicted [in trouble]? let him pray. Is any merry [happy]? let him sing psalms [praise]. ¹⁴ Is any sick [weary or weak] among you? let him call for the elders of the church; and let them pray over him, anointing him with oil in the name of the Lord: ¹⁵ And the prayer of faith shall save [heal] the sick, and the Lord shall raise him up; and if he have committed sins, they shall be forgiven him. ¹⁶ Confess your faults one to another, and pray one for another, that ye may be healed. The effectual fervent prayer of a righteous man availeth much. ¹⁷ Elias was a man subject to like passions as we are, and he prayed earnestly that it might not rain: and it rained not on the earth by the space of three years and six months. ¹⁸ And he prayed again, and the heaven gave rain, and the earth brought forth her fruit.

James forms his concluding remarks by reflecting back on how he began his epistle. He encourages believers to not forget the power of prayer and praise. Trials will come just as our Lord Jesus said; but He also said He would go through those trials with us! Prayer and praise are the prescription James gives to help us persevere. In the end, if we have effectively prayed and given the

Lord the praise due His name, we will have persevered until the end. This is our Lord's goal for us and it should also be ours. While we can and most certainly will sin along the way, our sin can and will be forgiven as we seek the Lord in honesty and sincerity. We can experience spiritual and physical healing as we confess our sin and seek God's deliverance. Let's explore this great subject of prayer and its power.

Prayer can simply be defined as talking to God. This blessed opportunity is only for humans as animals are not afforded this prospect. The Scriptures are replete with examples of prayer. Prayers can be offered in the way of requests for others or ourselves. Prayer can be both individual and corporate.

Prayer is a great privilege! Just think for a moment about the right of prayer. The Almighty Creator of everything has allowed believers to petition Him with prayer! God, who is absolutely sovereign, has decided to allow you and I to have a say in certain matters! He has done so through prayer. There are many circumstances the Scriptures say can be affected by prayer: nations can be changed, demonic forces stopped, mountains moved, sickness healed, attitudes transformed, minds changed, faith strengthened, sins forgiven, wisdom imparted, and many other situations can be affected as a result of prayer. When you stop to think about it, we should praise God for His decision to allow us to shape His creation! He is love, and because of this most glorious attribute, He has chosen to include men and women in the administration of world affairs via prayer. Truly, all good gifts come from above (1:18)!

For the Christian who has the end goal of the *crown of life* in view, prayer is absolutely essential! As we ponder the state of our Christian life, consider the following statement:

Christians are strongest when prayerful and weakest when prayerless.

How true these words are! When we consider our Lord's instruction to His disciples, He frequently taught them to pray. He rarely taught them how to preach or teach. Nor did they ask Him to do so. But they did ask Him to teach them how to pray.

Prayer is communing with God. However, it is not simply a one way communication line. God has spoken through His Word. As we meditate upon His Word, we can then offer prayers to Him. It is best to couple Biblical meditation and prayer. They truly go hand in hand. As we contemplate God's will revealed in His precious Word, we are then in a position to commune with Him. This does not mean we should never pray without reading His Word. It does mean the goal of prayer should be to fellowship with God – both hearing Him and being heard by Him.

Jesus himself was a man of daily prayer (Mark 1:35; 6:46). He was dependent upon His Father's instruction. He many times referred to the will of His Father and the importance of adherence to His Father's will. Jesus was in constant contact with His Father. Up until the cross, a moment did not go by when their fellowship was broken. Jesus' will was the Fathers' will. Jesus knew the Father's will was best, and He did not question His Father's provision or wisdom. He simply trusted His Father. Great love and contentment was His because of His special fellowship with His Father.

James was very aware of the power of prayer, especially in light of the various trials Christians face. He began the epistle with trials and prayer as important subjects (1:2-8). His entire epistle brings to light the struggle believers face; the purpose for the struggle (maturity); the way to be victorious (to persevere); and the goal of struggle and maturity – winning the *crown of life*! It is very fitting that James concludes his epistle with these same topics.

Succinctly, James tells us to pray if we are experiencing trouble. As believers in Jesus Christ, we have immense power upon which we can draw. The trials of our lives are ordained by God for our good and His glory. The way we endure trials is to rely on the power of our Lord. One important way we do this is through prayer. Prayer undergirds our perseverance. It allows us to express our feelings and desires to the Lord. As we do so, we are encouraged by His comforting hand. We are able to manage the trials by having a deep, purposeful, and enduring prayer life.

The importance of daily, planned prayer cannot be overemphasized. As already mentioned, daily prayer was the practice of Jesus. Daniel is an Old Testament example of a prayerful saint. Scores of other Biblical examples for prayer can be given. Nonetheless, many Christians are weak in the area of prayer. Why? A lack of faith. Prayer is communication with a God who cannot be physically seen or touched. While this may be true at present, He can be seen and touched by faith. Our Great High Priest (Heb 4:12-16) and Advocate (1 John 2:1) is seated on the throne at the right hand of the Father! He is ready, willing, and able to deliver us from any and all trouble. Bottom line, we must by faith prevail in prayer if we are to be victorious in our trials.

Praise to God is another action prescribed by James. While we certainly go through various trials, we are not always in trouble or in distress. Valleys are part of our lives, but mountain tops are also part of the journey. God is pleased when we praise

Him in the valley and on the mountain top. In turn, we are satisfied and fulfilled as we do so. Praise is the anthem of the ages. When we consider our ultimate purpose, praising God is at the center (cf. Rev 4-5).

Prayer and praise certainly go together. Our Lord's instruction for prayer in Matt 6:9 tells us to first honor and praise our Father whose name is hallowed! The book of Psalms is a book of prayer and praise. The very familiar Psalm 100 explains the role of praise precisely:

> ^{1} Make a joyful noise unto the LORD, all ye lands. ^{2} Serve the LORD with gladness: come before his presence with singing. ^{3} Know ye that the LORD he is God: it is he that hath made us, and not we ourselves; we are his people, and the sheep of his pasture. ^{4} Enter into his gates with thanksgiving, and into his courts with praise: be thankful unto him, and bless his name. ^{5} For the LORD is good; his mercy is everlasting; and his truth endureth to all generations.

As we contemplate God's grace and mercy towards us, we must praise Him! The practice of praise will help us avoid the delusion of depression. Focusing upon God's goodness and plan for our lives enables us to shout louder on the mountain tops and endure the lonesomeness of the valley. Depression is a very real adversary. Through prayer and praise we can avoid going deeper into the valley than necessary. James helps us see these truths as he brings his loving instruction to a close.

Next, James deals with prayer for those who are sick or weak in v. 14-15. His meaning seems to be physical sickness but can certainly be applied to spiritual problems. James has outlined a number of spiritual deficiencies among his readers throughout the epistle. While it is not always the case, sin can cause physical sickness. The laws of sowing and reaping definitely apply in the spiritual realm which sometimes translate into physical ailments. However, we must be careful not to make this a rule, as many times sickness has another purpose (cf. John 9:1-3; 11:5). While all sickness can ultimately be traced back to the original sin of Adam, all sickness is not the result of specific sins committed by an individual believer. Many wonder if God is punishing them with sickness because of some specific sin. He is not necessarily doing so, as good and bad things happen to all people. The rain falls on the just and the unjust (Matt 5:45). Also, God forgives sin when a Christian confesses sin as 1 John 1:9 tells us. While we do reap what we sow, if we confess our sin, God will forgive and fellowship will be restored.

	James' instruction is in the context of a local body of believers where someone may have a physical ailment. If so, the elders of the church are to pray and anoint the sick with oil. To be an elder demands wisdom. Elders are supposed to be mature spiritual leaders in a local body of believers. As such, their prayer should have power with God as they are to be in close communion with Him knowing His Word and will. The anointing with oil has a spiritual aspect in that it is symbolic of the Holy Spirit. But the purpose for the oil was most likely medicinal in nature. Plant based oils, such as Frankincense, had great medical value during this time period. Even today, essential oils such as Frankincense are used as natural antibiotics. Lavender oil is used for various maladies including burns. James does not discount the use of these oils to aid in the healing process.

Also, notice James' order where the sick person is to call for the elders. If requested, the elders are to oblige, praying in faith for the sick person. The prayer of faith is not something mystical. Rather, it is simply petitioning God, believing He is the Great Healer. James dealt with the subject of praying in faith in 1:5-6 when he said, we should ask for wisdom without doubting God's willingness and ability to give us wisdom. In the same fashion, the elders are to pray with wisdom and faith for the healing of members of the church who so request. Naturally, we must realize this is not a prescription for healing 100% of the time. All prayers are conditioned on the will of God concerning any matter. Having faith in God does not mean we put words into His mouth. Nor does it mean we can ask God for something and He is then obligated to give it to us. Requesting God's action must be done with humility and respect. It may not be God's will for the healing. The ultimate way to petition God is to acknowledge His goodness and sovereignty. When we do so, we can echo the prayer of the Lord Jesus when faced with the horrific prospect of the cross, *nevertheless, not as I will, but as thou wilt* (Matt 26:39b).

When the elders approach a request for healing with God, they must keep in mind God's revealed will. He has not said all will be healed in this life. Rather, He has said to ask in faith, knowing He can heal if He wills to do so. Hence, James' words must be taken in context with other Scripture concerning prayer and healing.

If a sinning believer has approached the elders of the church and requested prayer for healing, he has most likely recognized his sin and is willing to confess it in order that he can receive healing. While some may have no sin, they obviously are seeking the help of their spiritual leaders. It is also important we recognize James does not say all have sinned with sickness being the result. Rather he says sin is a possibility, but not a definite.

In verse 16, James gives a command unique to the New Testament – to confess faults to one another. We must recognize the background of this statement. James has dealt with various behavioral problems in the church. Many of the believers have sinned against one another. The result of this sinning has quite possibly resulted in sickness. The cure for the sickness is confession of sin and a petition to God for healing.

The confession of sin to a brother or sister in the Lord lies within the context of a sin committed against a brother or sister in the Lord. James does not instruct believers to confess private sins to one another. Our confession of sin should be to the extent of its influence. Private sin should be confessed privately to God. Sin against another believer should be confessed to that believer. Public sin requires public confession. We are to all have a forgiving spirit ready and willing to forgive the greatest infraction committed by our brothers and sisters in Christ (cf. Eph 4:30-32). We should all be praying for one another so that spiritual maturity and healing will be the end result.

James next tells us in the later part of verse 16 the prayers of a *righteous man* are powerful. They are powerful because God's power is unleashed many times via prayer. By a *righteous man*, James means more than simply a person who has experienced the new birth possessing judicial righteousness before God. The righteousness to which James refers is practical righteousness. Hence, the person who is judicially righteous, living his life in God's will (a doer of the Word and not a hearer only, 1:22) is a very powerful person!

The example of righteous Elijah is given to show how present day believers can be mighty in prayer. James reminds us Elijah was an ordinary man. He was not the Son of God without sin. Rather he was a sinner who had been saved by God's grace and was obediently following the Lord's instruction. Elijah was a man who conducted his life righteously, and God honored his actions. James' point is that everyday believers can petition the Lord for various matters and receive answers to their prayers.

The phrase *prayed earnestly* is literally "prayed with prayer." Elijah prayed; he really prayed with passion. His passion was rooted in God's will and Word. God had revealed His will to Elijah (1 Kings 18) who persisted in prayer for rain to stop but then 3 ½ years later for rain to fall. Elijah was able to pray in faith because he knew God's will. The same is true today. We should use God's Word as our guide for petitioning Him. Knowing God's will, as revealed in His Word, is the sure foundation for effective fervent prayer.

On a side note, it is helpful to know a little tradition regarding the writer James. His nickname is purported to have been "Camel Knees." He earned this title because of his consistent and persistent practice of prayer. It is said he would enter the temple alone to intercede for the forgiveness of the people so often that his knees became as hard as camel's knees. May we all follow this great example of power through prayer. Persisting in prayer pleases our Lord and will help assure us of the goal of our faith – the *crown of life*!

DISCUSSION QUESTIONS AND IDEAS

- Discuss the statement regarding the relationship between our spiritual strength and our prayer life.
- Discuss various approaches to remaining prayerful.
- Explain the power of prayer and praise.
- Study the life and actions of Elijah.
- Explain the importance of knowing the context of the passage where we are told to confess our faults.

CHAPTER 25
LOVE RESTORES

James 5:19-20

^{19} Brethren, if any of you do err [wander] from the truth, and one convert him; ^{20} Let him know, that he which converteth the sinner from the error of his way shall save a soul [life] from death, and shall hide a multitude of sins.

These final two verses of James' are powerful. Addressed to believers, James encourages them in the faith. He tells them to watch out for one another. He explains that a brother or sister in the Lord can wander away from the truth of God's Word. Love for the Lord as well as our brothers and sisters in Christ should compel us to reach out to those in error. The good news is that if we get off the path, we can get back on it. Our Lord is ready to forgive and restore us to fellowship.

It is always important to recognize to whom any writer addresses his message. Here, James' final address is to the *Brethren*. As we have noted throughout the epistle, James is speaking primarily to born again believers in the Lord Jesus Christ. James' final instruction is one that shows the very real possibility of a Christian being in moral error. Moral error many times results from theological error. If our theology is lacking, we can find ourselves backsliding into error. James notes that if one on the *brethren errs* or wanders *from the truth*, someone who is his brother or sister in the Lord should seek to restore him. This is not limited to the elders or the pastor. All of us should watch out for each other.

As noted in verse 16, we should all pray for one another. Verses 19 and 20 are the final thoughts from James as he concludes the epistle. They finalize the subject of prayer, forgiveness, and restoration begun in verse 13. Love and restoration are so characteristic of our Lord. Paul declared the Lord Jesus Christ's mission was one of reconciliation and restoration (2 Cor 5:18-19). Paul also stated Christians have been given the ministry of reconciliation in 2 Cor 5:18.

Restoration is the primary teaching of James 5:19-20. James wants us to *know* that our efforts for restoration are crucial. If we love the Lord and our brothers and sisters in Christ, we should be about the ministry of restoration. Love is not afraid to confront sticky issues. Many times Christians stray and begin to backslide. The answer many give for those who stray deeply into sin is that they were never Christians in the first place. While there are many who are church members but who are not Christians (only because they have never simply believed in Christ alone), James is not dealing with them. It should be clear from this first New Testament book that actions or works are not the evidence or even proof of the new birth. Quite the contrary, the actions of the *brethren* which James describes are less than glamorous. Jealousy, pride, infighting, foolishness, worldly pursuits, a love of money and status, and several other characteristics are what James addresses. He tells these brethren to stop doing these things. So yes, *brethren* can err from the truth – the truth of Scripture. *Brethren* need to allow the *word of truth* to continue its transformational work, making them more like

Christ. The truths concerning the *crown of life* James has revealed should motivate believers to seek it at all costs (just as Jesus instructed in Matt 6:33). Nonetheless, any believer can wander away from this truth and become disillusioned. James says we should be on the lookout for each other. To a certain extent we are our brother's keepers.

One of the reasons for the local church is protection. It is important believers are on the lookout for one another. When we see a fellow believer wandering, we can and should prayerfully seek to *convert* them back to fellowship with the Lord. In James' immediate context, it may involve confession of sin. They may have committed a public sin requiring public confession. A fellow believer can even be upset with another believer unjustly. Upon learning of the problem, the innocent believer should seek out the one who is upset and seek to reconcile. Obviously, such contact should be done in much love and humility. Encouraging fallen believers is very important. They must know there is forgiveness from God as well as their brothers and sisters in the Lord. In Galatians 6:1-2 Paul said:

> [1] Brethren, if a man be overtaken in a fault, ye which are spiritual, restore such an one in the spirit of meekness; considering thyself, lest thou also be tempted. [2] Bear ye one another's burdens, and so fulfil the law of Christ.

Paul's instruction is both loving and humbling. He tells us to fulfill the Law of Christ. The Law of Christ is summed up in one word – LOVE. Jesus gave a final command to His disciples that summed up His teaching:

> ³⁴ A new commandment I give unto you, That ye love one another; as I have loved you, that ye also love one another. ³⁵ By this shall all *men* know that ye are my disciples, if ye have love one to another. (John 13:34-35)

Just as God is love (1 John 4:10) operating in the mode of love, so should we. We should imitate God. Loving one another certainly means speaking kindly, serving, and giving to one another. However, loving one another also means we are willing to get "dirty" sometimes. Dealing with error and believers who have strayed is not always pleasant. It is many times messy, dirty work. But this was the work our Lord performed and so should we. So, as we go about our way, we must be willing to help our brethren who are in need, no matter the need. It may be a phone call to encourage, a lunch to hear of troubles, a visit to a home to confront, or various other scenarios. We must simply be available and spiritual enough to carry on this most important ministry.

We should also know restoration is a very real possibility. Prayer and diligent work via the *word of truth* can yield great restorative results. We should never give up on one another. The result James outlines is the saving of a soul from death and the covering of a multitude of sins.

As we have noted before, James' reference to saving a soul from death should be properly understood. In speaking to the *brethren* about the *brethren*, we should immediately recognize salvation from the lake of fire is not at stake. Rather, the saving of a soul from death ultimately refers to delivering one from the loss of reward and its consequences. Let's explore this subject a bit more in James' context.

The word *soul* is the Greek word *psuche*. It can be translated either "soul" or "life". It should be distinguished from the Greek word *pneuma* which is translated "spirit". Man is made up of body, soul, and spirit — He is Trichotomous. The soul is described in Scripture as the home of the mind, will, and emotion. It is the place where we live mentally and emotionally. We tend to experience life via our soul.

James is telling us that broken fellowship with God is death. If our fellowship remains in this state of death, we will not experience life as God intends. We know Paul and John spoke of believers committing sin to such an extent that God took their physical life as a result (1 Cor 11:30; 1 John 5:16). Sin of this nature caused God to judge these believers for their wicked conduct. Such behavior is not pleasing to God and will result in shame when these believers stand before the Lord at the Judgment Seat of Christ (1 John 2:28). This judgment will determine our "reward life" for eternity. Those who err and walk contrary to the Lord will not experience life as God intended and will in a sense face death — loss of reward. Those who are judged negatively by the Lord will never have the privilege of reigning alongside the Messiah Jesus in His kingdom. They will experience the shame a life lived in the flesh produces. They will not hear *well done* because they will not have done well. The parable of the talents in Matt 25 describes the outcome for an unfaithful believer in verses 24-30. This type of death is what James warns against and wants believers to avoid.

Knowing the great prospect for reward should radically change our thinking. We should be totally immersed in the *word of truth* allowing it to mature us. When we do so, our faith will reach its intended goal. As mature believers, we will naturally love others and want them to experience God's best. As James has revealed, God's great desire for every believer is the *crown of life*. Missing this reward will be devastating. May we be theologically correct allowing our theology to shape and direct our daily lives! God loves us and wants us to never face death relative to the *crown of life*. Trials may bring temporary sorrow, but endurance through the trials brings eternal reward. Yes, Perseverance Pays! Make sure you take this great encouragement from James and win the *crown of life*!

DISCUSSION QUESTIONS AND IDEAS

- Discuss Jesus' ministry of restoration.
- Discuss the love we should have for each other.
- Explain why it is so important that we rescue a backslidden brother or sister in Christ.
- Discuss the function of the soul.
- Discuss the various facets of death (you may want to refer back to Chapter 3).

Perseverance Pays

CHAPTER 26
ENCOURAGEMENT

James 1:12

Blessed is the man that endureth temptation: for when he is tried, he shall receive the crown of life, which the Lord hath promised to them that love him.

James 5:7-9

[7] Be patient therefore, brethren, unto the coming of the Lord. Behold, the husbandman waiteth for the precious fruit of the earth, and hath long patience for it, until he receive the early and latter rain. [8] Be ye also patient; stablish your hearts: for the coming of the Lord draweth nigh. [9] Grudge not one against another, brethren, lest ye be condemned: behold, the judge standeth before the door.

In this final chapter we want to summarize as well as emphasize James' overarching theme: perseverance pays! God has graciously promised great things for those who love Him! Knowing God understands the difficulties we face is a great comfort! Knowing He is going to reward us for our labor of love is a great motivator as well as a marvelous encouragement!

In 1:12, James assures us we will receive the *crown of life* for enduring temptation. The word for *endure* is the Greek word *hupomeno*. It means to bear trials, to have fortitude, to persevere. Hence, we know trials and temptations will come. As we have learned, trials are the tools God uses to shape and mold us into wise mature servants. As we bear the trials, we know the Lord is at work in our lives. He is making us into what will one day be beautiful in His sight. James 5:7-9 encourages us to be *patient*. We are to forbear, persevering through the trials of this life. He also proclaims the Lord is coming! Great hope and encouragement are ours as we look forward to our Lord's return! We know the trials of this life will come to an end. We also know our Lord is at work in our lives; He will faithfully complete what He started (cf. Phil 1:6). What an encouragement to know the purpose and end result of our journey of faith! God's ultimate purpose in our lives is to bless us with a regal crown for our head, a royal throne as our seat, and a stately inheritance for our possession! God's grace is truly amazing!

As we conclude our study of James, it is fitting to reflect upon what Jesus taught on this subject of reward or payment for perseverance. The Lord Jesus spoke frequently about the subject of rewards. In fact, Jesus strongly encouraged – even commanding – His followers to seek rewards. Some feel it is self-serving to seek rewards. However, this attitude is in contradiction to the teaching of the Lord Jesus Christ! He wants all believers to seek reward. As we shall see, reward is part of God's grand plan to show forth His marvelous grace.

In the famous Sermon on the Mount, Jesus spoke to His disciples about how they were to conduct their lives as His followers. The Sermon on the Mount is not a treatise on how to become a child of God (to be born again). Rather, it is direct

Encouragement

instruction from the Lord Jesus Christ on how to live our lives in a manner pleasing to God. Notice Jesus' doctrine in the beatitudes:

> ³ Blessed are the poor in spirit: for theirs is the kingdom of heaven. ⁴ Blessed are they that mourn: for they shall be comforted. ⁵ Blessed are the meek: for they shall inherit the earth. ⁶ Blessed are they which do hunger and thirst after righteousness: for they shall be filled. ⁷ Blessed are the merciful: for they shall obtain mercy. ⁸ Blessed are the pure in heart: for they shall see God. ⁹ Blessed are the peacemakers: for they shall be called the children of God. ¹⁰ Blessed are they which are persecuted for righteousness' sake: for theirs is the kingdom of heaven. ¹¹ Blessed are ye, when men shall revile you, and persecute you, and shall say all manner of evil against you falsely, for my sake. ¹² Rejoice, and be exceeding glad: for great is your reward in heaven: for so persecuted they the prophets which were before you. (Matt 5:3-12)

In these verses Jesus describes a Spirit filled believer – one who is in fellowship with the Lord and walking in victory. A striking fact should be apparent: victory in this life involves a fight which usually involves suffering. This passage describes the blessings awaiting those who faithfully persevere. Verse 3 proclaims those who are humble will possess the *kingdom of heaven*. Verse 5 describes the meek as those who *inherit the earth*. Both of these rewards describe a form of ownership faithful believers will have in the future kingdom of God. Verse 12 describes the outlook such a person should have: exceeding gladness and joy should be the outlook of the person Jesus describes. Why? Because reward in heaven (in the heavenly realm) awaits those who are persecuted for His sake! Notice He did not say the reward of heaven, but reward *in* heaven.

Further in the sermon, Jesus directs His disciples to pray and give with the proper motive. If they heed His words, reward is promised (cf. Matt 6:1-6). Again in Chapter 6 Jesus encourages His disciples to:

> [19] Lay not up for yourselves treasures upon earth, where moth and rust doth corrupt, and where thieves break through and steal: [20] But lay up for yourselves **treasures in heaven**, where neither moth nor rust doth corrupt, and where thieves do not break through nor steal" [Emphasis mine] (Matt 6:19-20).

Jesus did not say layup treasures in order to get to heaven. He said to lay them up *in* heaven. In order to lay up treasures in heaven, it is understood one must have a heavenly account in which to place the treasures. Also, notice the use of the plural *treasures*. Jesus is teaching His disciples to make **lasting investments** in the bank of heaven. He knows believers will be in heaven (they have an account[1] in heaven and will reside in heaven) and wants them to realize the importance of having **wealth** in heaven.[2] The idea of wealth in heaven is another way

---

[1] Paul uses this terminology and concept in Phil 4:17.
[2] The idea of wealth in heaven is difficult for some. However, the Scriptures teach there will be different degrees of privilege and responsibility

of describing reward (or the *crown of life* as James portrays). Again, according to the Lord Jesus, it is not selfish to seek treasures or wealth in heaven. In fact, He commands us to do so! Wealth in heaven is the will of God for every believer. It is God's plan to reward faithfulness with things *eye hath not seen, nor ear heard, neither have entered into the heart of man.* (1 Cor 2:9) Whether all believers will heed Jesus' advice and fulfill God's will is up to them. Believers should desire to be victorious in order to gain the riches of the world to come (cf. Heb 11:6, 26).

Later in Matthew, shortly after Peter's famous proclamation of Jesus being the *Christ, the son of the living God,* Jesus described the reward awaiting those who followed Him in obedience. Those believers who would be willing to take up their cross and follow Him in discipleship would be rewarded for their actions. Jesus proclaimed,

> ^{27} For the Son of man shall come in the glory of his Father with his angels; and then he shall **reward every man according to his works.** ^{28} Verily I say unto you, There be some standing here, which shall not taste of death, till they see the Son of man coming in his kingdom. [Emphasis mine] (Matt 16:27-28)

---

among those in heaven. All believers are encouraged to seek the imperishable riches in the ages to come. Sadly, not all believers seek these riches, but instead seek the temporal riches of the current age.

Notice, reward according to works is closely tied to the future kingdom. This fact is also observed in the beatitudes cited earlier.

In Matt 19:27-30, the disciples were wondering what benefit they would receive in exchange for their commitment to following Jesus. Jesus told them they would reign in the millennial kingdom with Him over the nation of Israel. He went on to say **anyone** who forsook earthly pleasures in exchange for service to Him would be over-compensated. Jesus promised a return on investment of 100 times (this represents a 10,000% rate of return). His answer need not be understood in an absolutely literal fashion. Jesus was simply saying the reward for faithful service is immense. In fact, the reward of God is a display of His marvelous grace being much more than we deserve!

In Matt 24:42-47, Jesus used a short parable to describe His intent to reward the *wise and faithful* servant with rulership over His entire domain (cf. Rev 3:21)! Later in Matt 25:14-30, via another parable, Jesus describes how He will judge His servants for the work they accomplished with the talents He gave them. Rulership over much[3] is promised for those who are obedient. Notice the servants are already His servants as Jesus is describing how He will judge the works of Christians. This judgment is

---

[3] Notice the difference in commendation, privilege, and responsibility between the two parables. In Matt 24:42-47, the servant is called *faithful and wise* and the resulting reward is rulership over all. In Matt 25:14-30, the obedient servant is called *good and faithful* and is ruler over much, but not all. Further delineation can be seen in the parable of the pounds in Luke 19:11-26, where Jesus addresses the obedient servant as a *good servant* and rewards him with rulership over cities. Thus, a difference in commendation, privilege, and responsibility is noted. Different degrees of obedience and faithfulness will be rewarded accordingly by our Righteous Judge.

relative to the works of these servants not involving the gift of eternal life. It should be noted that rulership is denied for the disobedient. Thus, rulership alongside Christ is a reward (recompense or payment) for faithfulness. It must not be confused with the gift of eternal life, which is a free gift. There are numerous other passages in the gospels which testify further of Jesus' teaching on reward. However, let's explore His comments after His resurrection. Please turn your attention to the book of Revelation for more of Jesus' teaching on reward.

In the Revelation Chapters 2-3, Jesus speaks directly to seven New Testament churches. The subject is their **performance** as believers. They are to remain faithful, producing good works. Jesus identifies their strengths and weaknesses. To each of the churches Jesus proclaims, *I know thy works*. To six of the seven churches, Jesus counsels them to heed His correction. Only one of the churches escapes a direct rebuke from the Lord. To this church, the church at Philadelphia, Jesus warns them to remain faithful by saying:

> Behold, I come quickly: hold that fast which thou hast, that no man take thy crown. (Rev 3:11)

These believers are to make sure they remain faithful in order to retain their reward – *the crown of life*. We all should take notice of these words. If we are currently faithful, we should not grow weary in well doing. We should pay attention to Jesus' words and guard our *crown*. It is much more valuable than we can really imagine! It must be noted again, Jesus is speaking to believers. He is evaluating their performance. He tells them if they will overcome,[4] He will reward them with special commendations, positions, and privileges. These blessings are certainly on the forefront of His mind as he counsels these churches. Jesus definitely wants His children to experience fullness and joy in His kingdom! He does not want anything to stand in their way. Rewarding faithful believers will one day "make" Jesus' day! Declaring *well done* will bring our Lord much joy and satisfaction. When complete, His work in our lives will be something He enjoys for all eternity as we praise and worship Him, admiring His wonderful plan!

For the overcoming Christian, Jesus reveals special rewards of intimacy, position, and privilege with Him in these two chapters from the Revelation. The Lord Jesus Christ greatly desires for every believer to overcome in order to share eternal privilege and intimacy. His directive to persevere and overcome shows our Lord's desire to give His children blessings. **This is at the heart of His teaching on reward; it is also where James' teaching on reward for perseverance emanates.**

Please realize the overwhelming privilege of co-rulership alongside the Lord Jesus Christ during His reign! Imagine the privilege of being at the King's table serving Him in an all important role! Envision serving at the "right hand" of the Lord!

---

[4] Some would argue all Christians are already overcomers citing 1 John 5:4. However, the type of overcoming Jesus encourages in Revelation is not something He has already accomplished for Christians. Christians have already overcome in one aspect through the work of Christ on their behalf (a positional aspect of overcoming). The admonition to overcome in Revelation is practical in nature and not positional in nature. Those who have overcome positionally are to then go on and overcome practically. Thus, to overcome positionally does not guarantee one will overcome practically.

Think about how Jesus will rule the earth in righteousness, love, and mercy! His reign will be the very opposite of Satan's current reign of terror. Then envision being an integral part of Jesus' rule! Some are saved yet satisfied with just having a home in heaven. While heaven is a wonderful place, it is not the only thing we are to focus upon. Simply going to heaven is not God's comprehensive will for us. It is far greater! God wants to bless us with glory, honor, and splendor beyond our imagination! Deliberate upon Jesus giving you direct orders to administer His will on earth. Realize yourself as a member of the royal aristocracy of the sky! Pondering these truths allows us to see by faith what lies in store for those who love the Lord!

In John Chapter 14, Jesus describes a believer who is enjoying the fruit of close knit fellowship with the Lord. Notice His words:

> [21] He that hath my commandments, and keepeth them, he it is that loveth me: and he that loveth me shall be loved of my Father, and **I will love him, and will manifest myself** to him. [22] Judas saith unto him, not Iscariot, Lord, how is it that thou wilt manifest thyself unto us, and not unto the world? [23] Jesus answered and said unto him, If a man love me, he will keep my words: **and my Father will love him, and we will come unto him, and make our abode with him.** [Emphasis mine] (John 14:21-23)

Jesus and the Father desire cherished love and fellowship with obedient believers. They want obedient believers to have an abundance of blessings. The most important of which is close knit shared experiences with the King, the Lord Jesus Christ, during His Messianic reign as well as the eternal ages. Sharing glory and splendor with faithful believers is our Lord's will.

In the last chapter of the Revelation, Jesus gives the final word to believers regarding reward:

> And, behold, I come quickly; and my reward is with me, to give every man according as his work shall be. (Rev 22:12)

SUMMARY OF MAJOR JUDGMENTS

#	JUDGMENT	WHO	WHEN	WHERE	BASIS	OUTCOME
1	The Cross	The Whole World: John 1:29; 3:16; 5:24	Approximately 33 AD	Earth – At Calvary	Work of God's Son	Gift of eternal life to everyone who believes – entrance into the kingdom.
2	Judgment Seat of Christ	All Church Dispensation Believers: Rom 14:10-12; 2 Cor 5:6-11	After the Rapture	Heaven – at the Bema	Works done on earth	Eternal reward or loss of eternal reward – Inheriting or not inheriting the kingdom. Positions in the kingdom determined.
3	Beast & False Prophet	Beast and False Prophet: Rev 19:11-20	After the tribulation – at the Revelation	Earth – at Messiah's Throne	Rejection of Christ; deceit of others	Eternal condemnation in the Lake of fire – high degree of punishment.
4	Israel	Living Jews: Mal 3:2-5; Ez 20:33-38; Matt 25:1-12	After the Revelation	Earth – at Messiah's Throne	Tribulation Israel's response to God	Unbelieving: Lake of fire with degrees of punishment. Believing: Kingdom entrance with degrees of reward or loss. Inheritance and positions in the kingdom determined.
5	Gentiles	Living Gentiles: Joel 3:1-2; Matt 25:31-46	After the Revelation – after #4	Earth – at Messiah's Throne	Tribulation Gentile's response to God	Unbelieving: Lake of fire with degrees of punishment. Believing: Kingdom entrance with degrees of reward or loss. Inheritance and positions in the kingdom determined.
6	OT & Tribulation Saints	All OT and Tribulation Saints (who died during the tribulation) Dan 12:1-3; Rev 20:4-6	After the Revelation	Earth – at Messiah's Throne	Works done on Earth	Eternal Reward or loss of eternal reward – Inheriting or not inheriting the kingdom. Positions in the kingdom determined.
7	Satan & Fallen Angels	Satan & Fallen Angels: Matt 25:41; Rev: 20:10	End of the millennium	In the heavens	Rebellion against God & evil works	Eternal torment in the lake of fire – highest degree of punishment.
8	Great White Throne	All yet unjudged – unbelievers and believers: Rev 20:11-15	After the millennium	In the heavens	Response to God as well as works done on earth	Unbelieving: Lake of fire with degrees of punishment. Believing: Degrees of reward or loss. Inheritance and positions in the eternal kingdom determined.

Made in the USA
Columbia, SC
08 September 2019